Seven Indicators That Move Markets

Seven Indicators That Move Markets

Forecasting Future Market Movements for Profitable Investments

Paul Kasriel
Keith Schap

McGraw-Hill
New York   Chicago   San Francisco
Lisbon   London   Madrid   Mexico City
Milan   New Delhi   San Juan   Seoul
Singapore   Sydney   Toronto

Library of Congress Cataloging-in-Publication Data

Kasriel, Paul L.
    Seven indicators that move markets / Paul L. Kasriel, Keith Schap.
        p.   cm.
    ISBN 0-07-137013-7
    1. Investment analysis. I. Schap, Keith.   II. Title.

HG4529.K37   2001
332.6—dc21   2001044616

McGraw-Hill

A Division of The **McGraw·Hill** Companies

1 2 3 4 5 6 7 8 9 0   AGM/AGM   0 9 8 7 6 5 4 3 2

ISBN 0-07-137013-7

*This book was set in Palatino by Kim Sheran and Joanne Morbit of McGraw-Hill
Professional's Hightstown, N.J., composition unit.*

Printed and bound by Quebecor World/Martinsburg.

This publication is designed to provide accurate and authoritative information in regard to the subject matter covered. It is sold with the understanding that neither the author nor the publisher is engaged in rendering
legal, accounting, futures/securities trading, or other professional service.
If legal advice or other expert assistance is required, the services of a com-
petent professional should be sought.

*—From a Declaration of Principles jointly adopted by a Committee
of the American Bar Association and a Committee of Publishers*

*For Katy Kasriel
and Jim Schap*

Contents

Preface

The genesis of this book was a chart in the *Wall Street Journal* back in 1984 that Kasriel happened on during his morning train commute. This chart showed the relationship between the Treasury-bond–Treasury-bill yield spread and the stock market.

Kasriel, then an economist at the Federal Reserve Bank (FED) of Chicago, could hardly wait to call this chart to the attention of one of his Fed colleagues, Bob Laurent. The moment Kasriel entered Laurent's office, and before Kasriel could say a word, Laurent asked, "Did you see that chart in this morning's *Journal?*"

The reason for their excitement over this chart was that it was consistent with their view of how monetary policy works. At the same time, a mutual friend of theirs, Bob Keleher, who was then an economist at the Atlanta Fed, had been doing research on the use of market prices as a guide to monetary policy decisions.

Keleher's work had sensitized Laurent and Kasriel to this alternative approach to monetary policy decision making. And when Kasriel left the Fed for the "real world" of Fed watching at the Northern Trust Company, he used this market-indicators approach in assessing both the prospects for Fed policy actions and the effects of such actions. He incorporated the use of market indicators in weekly commentaries and speeches that he made.

Schap first heard Kasriel speak about the utility of market indicators early in 1990 at a conference he was covering for *Futures* magazine. This led to an article later that year and a continued use of these insights in a whole series of economic and market outlook articles.

Ultimately, Schap developed the volatility indicator on the basis of well-known option market information and put it together with the yield spreads and commodity index readings as key features of a "Market Insights" page that became a regular *Futures* department.

Later, as part of his work at the Chicago Board of Trade, Schap began to track the fed funds futures spreads. Over and over, these spreads have helped readers anticipate Fed policy changes. Indeed, this indicator proved useful enough that several publications picked it up and have continued to feature it.

With the passage of time, two things about the market indicators became more and more obvious. The market indicators provide information that allows forecasters and investors to anticipate general market events most of the time. Indeed, since November 1996, the Conference Board has included a variation of the yield spread as one of the components of its index of leading economic indicators. The average person can learn to use these indicators even without having had formal training in economics. Schap, after all, has had no course work in this field.

Because these indicators are based on data that anyone can find in newspapers or online, any investor who cares to spend a few hours reading this book and then a few hours more using this conceptual framework to study the markets can master them. In a relatively short time, the average investor should discover that study and use of the market indicators will enhance his or her ability to plan and implement imvestment strategies.

At a time when more and more people are taking responsibility for their retirement savings and other investments, these seem potentially valuable tools to make available. Hence this book.

1
Market Indicators for a New Investment Era

Investing has changed—at least insofar as market access and responsibility for decision making are concerned. Two factors seem to account for most of the change.

The gradual switch from defined-benefit corporate pension plans to defined-contribution employee savings plans shifted much of the investment choice from professional investment managers to individual investors. With choice comes responsibility for decision making about where to put the money. As 401(k) and other such defined-contribution plans have gained popularity, sponsors have increased the choices to the point where participants face some complex decisions.

At the same time that all this was going on, the increasing popularity of discount brokerages and, especially, Internet-based brokerages has caused transaction costs to dwindle. This puts "playing the market" well within the reach of more people than ever before. The most publicized, and probably most troubling, aspect of this development is that, for the first time, small-scale investors can feasibly day trade.

As with the shift from defined-benefit to defined-contribution plans with regard to retirement savings, the shift in the delivery of brokerage services assumes that investors will make their own investment decisions. Of course, the lower cost of trading online or through a discount broker is part of a trade-off in which investors pay less to invest but forgo access to the kind of research information and investment advice that full-service brokers provide.

This is wonderful. You're responsible for your own investment choices, but, while transaction costs have dwindled, you have fewer resources available to help you make such choices.

Or do you?

Few people have the resources and training the professional portfolio managers have in terms of an education in economics and finance. Yet this need not be a counsel of despair. Futures markets, as well as a number of similar market-like phenomena, serve as open-ended information generators. With small effort, you can learn to "read the markets" in a way that will help you derive a great deal of information that can be extremely useful in making investment decisions.

Who

If any of this description of the current investment climate fits your situation, you will find this book helpful. Even if the sum of your investment decision making involves no more than which of a half dozen or so mutual funds to route your 401(k) contributions into, this book can help you make those decisions on the basis of a good understanding of what the U.S. economy is likely to do in the coming months and how that might affect your retirement savings.

If, over the years, you have put together a private portfolio of mutual funds or individual stocks or are just getting started on such a project, you will find this book even more helpful. As you learn to use the futures markets to predict what the Federal Reserve (Fed) might do at its next several meetings and interpret the messages of the various yield curves, credit spreads, and commodity indexes and price arrays, you will begin to establish a basis for filtering the other information you use and for deciding which asset classes make more or less sense given your expectations for the economy. You will find ways to judge whether now is the time for growth or value stocks, small cap or large. Finally, considerations of volatility and other options-based information can help you plan shorter-term moves. If analysts are recommending buying on dips, you can use these probability-driven tools to estimate what constitutes a likely dip.

If you are planning a short-term trade, for whatever reason, these volatility tools can help you define the potential of the trade in probabilistic terms.

In short, any person who is serious about preparing a sound financial future and who enjoys thinking about what is going on in the economy, what is likely to happen next, and how to shape an investment strategy that will help him or her benefit from these expectations will find the discussions of this book intriguing and helpful.

The one category of person who will not find this book of interest is the group looking for a magic formula that will lead to instantaneous success on a staggering scale. We know of no such formula. The search for it reminds us of the legends about the search for untold riches that led explorers to the deserts of the American Southwest. The gold wasn't there, and the searchers ended up thirsty and, in many cases, dead.

The Legendary Perfect Trade

The personal finance magazines are full of stories about people making exactly the right move at exactly the right time and reaping untold riches. It seems a good idea to view these stories with more than slight skepticism.

There's a story that surfaces around the Chicago markets from time to time about a trader in the index option pits who made enough money during the 1987 crash to provide for a life of ease. This came about because he had managed to be long a huge number of puts on Standard & Poor's (S&P) 500 futures. A *put* is an option that gains in a down market, and the October S&P 500 market was real down.

Yet there's more to this story than meets the eye on first telling. It turns out that this man wasn't the least bit prescient. Rather, going into that fateful day, he'd been short a bunch of puts (that is, he'd sold them), which would have been ruinous in a down market. In his panic over the situation he saw developing that day, he tried to offset it, but he accidentally went long a large multiple of the number he meant to. When the smoke cleared, he found his mistake had made him a wealthy man.

The details of this trade have never surfaced, but here is one way it could have played out. The S&P 500 dropped 58 index points on October 19, 1987. Suppose that the value of the option contract that man was trading changed 40.91 option points. To find the cash-equivalent value of this change, multiply the point change by $250 to learn that one contract would gain or lose $10,227.50 (40.91 × $250 = $10,227.50). A position short 1,000 options contracts would have lost roughly $10.23 million that day. By inadvertently saying 10,000 instead of 1,000, this trader offset that loss, but he had 9,000 extra contracts that would have gained a total of $92.05 million ($10,227.50 × 9,000 = $92,047,500).

The frightening part of this situation, to the trader, was that he hadn't known what he was doing. He'd made a lucky mistake, but it could just as easily have gone the other way. Had he said 100 instead of 1,000 in his panicky state, 900 of his original 1,000 contracts would have remained in effect. He would then have lost $9.2 million ($10,227.50 × 900 = $9,204,750).

Needless to say, making such a $9.2 million mistake right would have posed a serious problem. After thinking this over and realizing how easily the outcome could have been tragic rather than happy, this trader took his money and ran. He gave up trading.

Patience, Persistence, and Probability

The people who seem to do the best, year in and year out, are the ones who are patient, persistent, and base what they do on their attempts to use high-probability strategies.

The agricultural schools impart a homely bit of advice to future farmers: "Plan your farm, and then farm your plan." The implicit message here is to stick with the plan. Don't listen to the siren songs that try to lure you into this or that can't-miss deal. Such songs too often lure you onto a rocky shore. When a strategy for investing has resulted from careful study and thought, be patient. Give it a chance to work.

A portfolio manager for a money management firm once pointed out to a neophyte reporter that he didn't get paid for being right about the markets. He got paid for being fully invested. For those of us operating on a smaller scale, this translates into sticking with the markets. A 401(k) plan enforces this for us. Every pay period, a certain amount of money gets invested. It doesn't always have to go to the same investments. At times, it makes sense to give more weight to one asset class than to another. But it should go somewhere.

Further, the professionals are no more sure of what will happen than any of the rest of us. They use all the information they can get to reduce the guesswork. They try to make moves that give them a relatively high probability of success. In one of his Hornblower novels, C. S. Forester has two of his characters say this about luck:

> "My heartiest congratulations on your success."
> "Thank you," said Hornblower. "I was extremely lucky ma'am."
> "The lucky man," said Lady Barbara, "is usually the man who knows how much to leave to chance."

Our goal in this book is to help you reduce how much you have to leave to chance.

Concrete, Public, and Forward-Looking

This isn't magic. While the U.S. government compiles and shares mountains of data about the U.S. and world economies, those data arrive after a considerable delay and are frequently revised. Even the most important statistics, such as the Consumer Price Index (CPI) or initial jobless claims, undergo revisions.

Almost any day you look you can find reports that include comments such as these:

- U.S. consumer prices rose 0.1 percentage point more than previously reported from December to August because the Bureau of Labor Statistics *erred in calculating* the cost of housing [italics added].
- August's orders by U.S. companies for domestic and imported machine tools totaled an estimated $480 million compared with a *revised* estimate of $453 million in July [italics added].

This makes these data hard to use for anyone, even those with extensive training and experience.

Public auction markets such as the futures markets, in contrast, establish market-clearing prices every day. These may change, too, but only because the situation has changed or people's perceptions of the situation have changed. These prices do not change because data were miscounted or erroneously calculated.

In addition, commodities trade in multiple contract months. While individual prices typically defy historical interpretation, the relationships between cash and futures prices—in market jargon, the *basis*—and between nearby and deferred futures prices—in market jargon, the *spread*—often reveal interesting and useful insights into the supply-demand dynamics of that market. Financial futures spreads can provide similarly useful information. These market indicators typically signal changing economic conditions well before other sources.

Reasons for this are not hard to find.

Futures markets are public places. Take fed funds. Only bank members of the Federal Reserve System can trade in the actual fed funds market. In contrast, anyone who can open a futures account can trade fed funds futures at the Chicago Board of Trade. The other futures markets, all over the world, are similarly open to investors with opinions and the money to back them.

As a result of this democracy of access, these markets attract people with different needs and different bits of information. No one person can know all there is to know about, say, the copper market. Manufacturers of wire or automotive components might have one piece of the knowledge puzzle. People with business connections in South America might have another piece.

A brief example shows how this can shape the prices you see on the quotation pages of a newspaper or on a computer screen. Consider a greatly simplified marketplace peopled only by Traders 1, 2, 3, and 4. Exhibit 1-1 shows the business focus of each trader, his or her special knowledge about the copper situation, his or her supply-demand expectation, and his or her market stance. The exhibit implies a causal sequence as you read from left to right.

These four people will adjust their bids and offers according to what they know and how that shapes their expectations relative to copper prices.

The bullish traders might be willing to pay up a bit at present because the current price might look reasonable compared with what they expect in a few months. As sellers, they may decide to

Exhibit 1-1 How Markets Bring Together Information

Trader	Connections	Special knowledge	Supply-demand expectations	Market view
1	Midwestern commercial real estate, construction	Numerous big projects on the drawing boards with firm tenant commitments	Emerging demand	Bullish
2	Business connections in Chile	Political pressures are easing	Supply surge	Bearish
3	Does business in Asia	Economies on the upswing, manufacturing heating up	Demand surge	Bullish
4	East Coast residential construction	Regional economy slow, little new housing in the pipeline	Shrinking demand	Bearish

wait for the higher prices they expect in the future. Either way, the bulls' actions will exert upward pressure on prices.

The bearish traders may be willing sellers now because they expect prices to drop in the future. They may also defer buying or buy for future delivery to take advantage of the lower prices they expect to see in a few months. Either choice will drive prices lower.

The schematic diagram of Exhibit 1-2 shows how the market activity of each trader will contribute to the shaping of the futures price that ultimately emerges as a result of this process.

The actual markets multiply these four traders by many thousands, of course, each with his or her own bit of information. The futures price that emerges results from a process of factoring all this together. Allowing for all these factors and views, the result is the market-clearing price for this moment. Additional news can motivate revisions.

Economists classify economic indicators as *leading, coincident,* and *lagging*. Obviously, only a leading indicator has utility for

Exhibit 1-2 Feeding Knowledge into the Futures Market

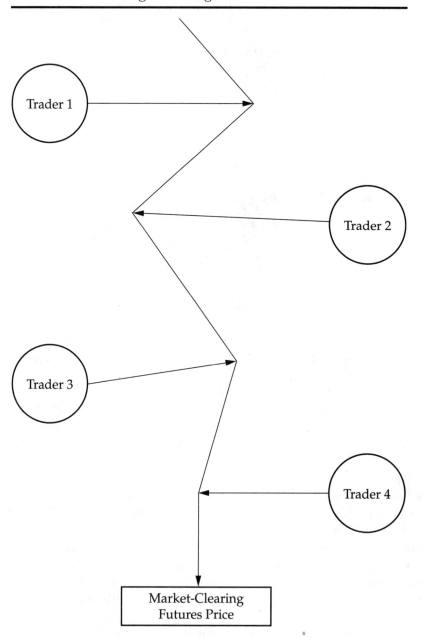

investors. If you only learn of something as it is happening, it is too late. You'll be buying high, which is not a good thing.

These market indicators tend to lead market events in useful ways. Partly, this is built into the nature of futures prices, and especially the complete arrays of contract-to-contract prices we focus on.

You can begin to see how this works if you consider the distinction between spot and forward prices. A *spot price* is the price for immediate, on-the-spot delivery, such as a retail price for, say, a computer. You pay the price and walk out with the goods. A *forward price*, in contrast, is a price you and another person agree on now for future delivery and payment.

Your willingness to pay a forward price depends on what you think the spot price is likely to be by the time you need the goods. If you think supplies will overwhelm demand and drive prices lower by then, you will be unwilling to pay a high forward price. Conversely, if you think supplies will be tight, you might agree to pay more now to avoid paying a great deal more later. Futures are standardized forward contracts, so, by their very nature, they incorporate this vital forward-looking aspect.

A Market Can't Think, or Maybe It Can

Throughout this book you will come across phrases such as "the market thinks" or "the market wants." A grammatical purist might object to this language on the grounds that a market is an inanimate object or an abstract idea. In neither case can it think, want, or anything else that takes human agency. If you think of a market in terms of a shopping mall or a futures or stock exchange trading floor, this objection seems well founded.

However, think of similar terms such as *college* or the Greek word for market, *agora*. Is a college the physical campus or rather the collection of scholars who gather to trade ideas? The term *college*, after all, derives from *collegium*, a group in which each member has approximately equal power and authority. Similarly, the term *agora* means, at root, a gathering or assembly, and our word *gregarious* comes from the same root.

In these discussions, then, the term *market* refers to the people who trade through a centralized forum, each with his or her own outlook, knowledge, and economic needs. A futures price pulls all this opinion and knowledge together and balances claim against claim to arrive at a market-clearing price that represents the collective wisdom of all the people who make up this market. To say "the market thinks" in this context is shorthand for a melding together of the views and knowledge of all these people.

A Glimpse at the Structure of This Book

The basic premise of this book is that you will do better when it comes to investment decision making if you have a good basic sense of how the U.S. economy will perform during the next few months. You want to know whether the economy will be growing or contracting. If the former, you want to know whether inflation will become a threat. And you want to know what kinds of investments will do better given whatever outlook you come up with.

Because the central bank holds the key to much of this, it seems a good place to start. We begin with an overview of the role of the Federal Reserve System (Fed) in terms of how it uses its power to create credit to control economic growth. In one view, the task of the Fed is to balance its base interest rate relative to a natural interest rate. Along with this, it is crucial to recognize the important distinction between transfer credit and created credit.

The next step is to see how you can use fed funds futures prices to tap into a helpful market consensus about what the Fed is likely to do during the next few months in terms of setting targets for monetary policy.

Following that, you will see how you can use various yield curves to assess demand for credit relative to the Fed-controlled supply of credit. After that, you will see how the credit spreads between default-free debt securities and defaultable debt securities, such as Treasury bills and Eurodollars or Treasury and agency notes, can help you evaluate the soundness of the credit being issued.

Turning from interest-rate markets to the markets for hard commodities, you will see how changes in commodity index prices can help you call turning points in economic cycles and also how commodity price arrays can help you anticipate changes in other economic sectors.

Volatility is an important factor in any market. Market professionals use volatility to gauge risk—and opportunity. An extremely agitated market obviously provides both opportunities and risks that a relatively quiescent one does not. The discussion here, though, focuses on how you can use volatility and other tools that derive from the options markets to estimate the probable extent of market movement relative to a specified time horizon. This will give you a way of putting a number to an analyst's comment that the stock market seems unlikely to move much farther up. You can define how far.

Unfortunately, market indicators can wear out. We discuss a series of indicators that seem to have lost effectiveness and offer hints, at least, about what might have happened to erode their utility. We mention another series of factors that make markets noisy enough to blur signals for shorter periods of time, such phenomena as the fabled Y2K effect.

Finally, having given hints about how this information can be used in investment decision making, we close with a slightly more thorough discussion of how we think you might put this information about the economy to work in your investment decision making.

A Suggestion about How to Use This Book

This isn't a novel. It won't ruin the ending if you read a later chapter sooner or don't read the book cover to cover.

If you share our fascination with these markets, you already gather a great deal of information from newspapers, magazines, radio and TV programs, investment newsletters, and conversations with a variety of people. You need all of this. Investing is complex enough that you need as much information as you can process.

This book can contribute in two ways. It will add to your store of knowledge, and it will provide a conceptual framework that will help you sort out and make sense of what others are saying about the markets and provide a sound basis for deciding where to put your investment dollars.

While you may prefer to read this book straight through to get the big picture, you should feel free to go to the parts that seem to offer the most immediate help—given the investment challenge of the moment. You can always go back to the other parts as they become relevant to you.

2
The Role of the Fed

Any investment story must start with an understanding of how the Federal Reserve System (Fed) operates and why it does what it does. From there, you can begin to appreciate what Fed policy shifts can mean to your investment strategies and to plan accordingly.

What matters most is that the Fed's primary charge is to govern monetary policy in such a way as to keep inflation under control and to ensure price stability. What this comes down to is that the Fed is the residual supplier of credit to the U.S. economy.

Conceptually, it is this simple. Say the Fed has decided to target a 6.50 percent fed funds rate, the only interest rate it can control. Next, consider what happens when demand for credit exceeds supply of credit. Interest rates will rise. Even the fed funds rate will have to rise. Given that the Fed wants to hold to the 6.50 percent target, it must, and will, supply enough credit to take care of the residual demand and to restore equilibrium in the credit markets.

Practically speaking, the Fed's task is anything but simple. For one thing, discussions of interest rates are rife with misunderstanding. In general, people seem to think that high interest rates are bad and low interest rates are good. But think about what really low interest rates mean. This is no definition of a financial Garden of Eden. Interest rates near the low end of the range could signal that corporations and individuals alike have little desire to buy anything. Interest rates are low because credit supply exceeds demand. This happens when nothing much is happening in the economy—hardly a good situation.

Conversely, higher interest rates could signal a relatively vibrant economy. Companies are spending to increase production capacity, individuals are buying the goods the companies are producing, and both corporations and individuals are borrowing to do so. As a result, competition for credit is forcing interest rates higher. At least to a point, then, higher interest rates are a sign of a thriving and growing economy.

The Fed's Balancing Act

The role of the Fed in all this becomes clearer in terms of the monetary theory of Knut Wicksell, a Swedish economist who published his classic *Interest and Prices* in 1898. Wicksell's theory turns on the notion that the task of a central bank is to find the balance between the market interest rate and a natural interest rate. In the United States, the market rate is the fed funds rate.

The central bank targets an interest rate that serves as the *base* rate on which rests the rest of the interest-rate structure. If the expected return on capital—in Wicksell's terms, the *natural* rate of interest—is above the interest-rate level the central bank is targeting, entrepreneurs will want to borrow more in order to earn the spread between the expected return on capital and their borrowing rate. What is the ultimate source of funds for these borrowing entrepreneurs? The central bank. The only way that the central bank can keep the base rate at its targeted level is for the central bank itself to supply more credit to the market. If the central bank persistently targets a base rate below the expected rate of return on capital, economic activity will continue to move up and ultimately lead to an overheated economy and higher inflation. If the central bank targets a base rate above the expected rate of return on capital, the opposite will occur. Entrepreneurs will cut back on their borrowing, economic activity will slow, and inflation will moderate.

So, all the central bank has to do to maintain a constant rate of inflation is to keep its base interest rate equal to the expected rate of return on capital—Wicksell's natural rate. Put this way, the task of the central bank in the Wicksellian scheme of things seems laughably simple. Nothing could be farther from the truth. Wicksell never assumed that the natural rate would hold constant through time. For one thing, new technologies tend to create new profit opportunities. Then the central bank needs to increase the natural rate. You can see that even if the central bank happened to set its base rate equal to the natural rate "today," the natural rate could rise "tomorrow," which would mean that yesterday's base rate is now too low.

What makes this even trickier is that, as Wicksell noted, the natural rate is not directly observable. Even though the central bank knows that new technology implies a change in the natural rate, it has no direct way of knowing either what the former natural rate was or what the new one is.

Assuming that the central bank wants to promote price stability, Wicksell's monetary policy rule was for the central bank to keep raising its base rate as long as commodity prices were rising. If commodity prices were falling, this was an indication that the base rate was above the natural rate and called for a central bank rate cut.

In today's "new era" economy, where services are a bigger factor than they were in Wicksell's time, traditional commodity prices may no longer be as reliable a guide concerning whether the base rate is above or below the natural rate. However, the central bank can derive another useful signal from the money supply numbers. If the base rate is below the natural rate, entrepreneurs will want to borrow more, and the central bank will be the ultimate supplier of that credit. In turn, the money supply will increase. The money supply will decrease if the central bank keeps the base rate above the natural rate.

Where the Government-Sponsored Enterprises Fit In

As technological changes have emerged, the financial markets have become more democratic and less nationalistic in many ways. A commonplace of the times is the observation that, in this Internet world, money knows no national boundaries. Certainly, the world's currency markets seem to support this conclusion. Still, things haven't gotten as democratic as some people worry they have.

A number of Congress people, U.S. Treasury officials, and financial commentators began worrying aloud during the latter part of 1999 that organizations such as Fannie Mae and Freddie Mac [technically, government-sponsored enterprises (GSEs), but agencies in financial market parlance] were getting too large and, among other things, had become runaway credit creators, directly or indirectly pumping up the economy and asset prices. Although there is no denying that GSEs have significantly increased their lending, this is another one of the misconceptions that cloud people's understanding of the credit markets. GSEs can only be a party to the creation of credit if the Fed willingly or unknowingly underwrites the credit.

The Credit World As Simple Stage

To understand why this is so, assume that the only transaction medium that exists is government-printed fiat currency. Further assume that there are no financial intermediaries—that is, ultimate borrowers deal directly with ultimate lenders. Suppose that there is an increased demand for funds because some bozo has the idea of selling books at a loss via the Internet. This increased demand for funding would put upward pressure on the structure of interest rates.

The higher level of interest rates would cause some other borrowers to cut back on the quantity of funds they now demand. Thus these borrowers would be cutting back on their spending so that this bozo with an Amazonian appetite for funds could increase his spending. The higher level of interest rates would cause some lenders to increase the quantity of funds they now are willing to supply, implying that they would be cutting back on their current spending.

In this case, where the increased demand for funding results in an increase in the level of interest rates, spending power would be transferred to the bozo from those who increased their lending and those who curtailed their borrowing. For the economy as a whole, there would be no net increase in spending.

Enter a GSE, Lending

The next institutional character in this little drama is a financial intermediary that has greater expertise in evaluating credit quality than does the average Joe or Jane on the street. Moreover, this intermediary is willing to offer the average Joe or Jane a menu of asset denominations and maturities. Assume, then, that all funds are advanced to the ultimate demander of them through this intermediary—call it a GSE, to make things simple.

Again, assume that demand for funds in the aggregate increases because of Bozo's hair-brained idea. Bozo goes to the GSE hat in hand. The GSE agrees to advance Bozo funds at some markup over the GSE's cost of funds. In order for the GSE to raise more funds, it has to offer higher interest rates. This induces some people to cut back on their current spending and place these additional "savings" with the GSE. Because the GSE's cost of funds has risen, it must increase the lending rate it is charging existing borrowers.

At the higher interest rate, some of these borrowers will cut back on the quantity of funds they are demanding. Notice that the end result is the same with the GSE intermediating as it was without a financial intermediary. That is, spending power is transferred to Bozo from others, resulting in no net increase in aggregate spending. The GSE has not created any additional credit.

Enter the Fed, Printing

To get closer to reality, assume that the central bank, call it Greenspan & Co., is targeting the level of an interest rate. Again, there is an increased aggregate demand for funds because of Bozo's scheme. Again, this puts upward pressure on the structure of interest rates, with or without a GSE. Unless Greenspan & Co. is willing to see its interest-rate target violated on the upside, it must create some additional credit by printing up some fresh currency and advancing it directly to Bozo or using it to purchase some other debt or equity in the economy.

In this case, spending power is not being transferred from others to Bozo. Rather, spending power is being created for Bozo. In the aggregate, spending does increase in this case.

What this should make clear is that GSEs cannot create spending power. Only the Fed can do that. So, if you think there is too much spending on goods, services, or assets in the U.S. economy, don't blame the intermediary; blame the primary source of credit creation—Greenspan & Co.

How the Fed Works

The Fed creates credit or reduces the supply of it through its policy arm, the Federal Open Market Committee (FOMC). This group has 12 voting members—the 7 members of the Board of Governors of the Federal Reserve and 5 Federal Reserve Bank presidents. The Fed chairman chairs the FOMC, and the president of the Federal Reserve Bank of New York is a permanent voting member and the vice chairman of the FOMC. While all 12 Federal Reserve Bank presidents attend and participate, only 5 vote, 1 permanent and 4 on a rotating basis. The FOMC conducts eight regularly scheduled meetings a year, although the group may confer by telephone much more often than that.

Exhibit 2-1 shows the schedules for 1998 through 2001 and includes the record of where the Fed set, or left, the fed funds target at each meeting to date and what it said about its bias.

You can see from Exhibit 2-1 that at 14 of the 22 FOMC meetings in 1998, 1999, and through October 2000, the Fed left its fed funds target unchanged. Notice that the announcement of bias was a new feature in 2000. The information had been available in recent years, but not this conveniently so.

A special feature of the 1998 series was the surprise 25-basis-point drop in the target on September 29. This surprised the market because the Fed seldom resets its target other than at its regularly scheduled meetings. The last time it had done so was in 1994. This shows that the Fed can do this when unusual circumstances warrant such a move. In September 1998, the unusual circumstances included the Russian credit default, the Long-Term Capital Management situation, and the threat these posed to the U.S. banking system.

You often see or hear comments from people who should know better that the Fed always moves its fed funds target in 25-basis-point increments. Don't believe this for a minute. Certainly, a 25-basis-point move is the norm, but the Fed bumped its target from 6.00 to 6.50 percent as recently as May 16, 2000. During the 300-basis-point tightening sequence that ran from February 1994 to February 1995, the Fed made three 50-basis-point moves and one 75-basis-point move.

The key outcome of these meetings, as far as most of the investment community is concerned, is what the Fed does with the fed

Exhibit 2-1 FOMC Meeting Schedules, Actions, and Biases

Announcement date	Fed funds target	Fed bias
Start of 1998	5.50	
February 4	5.50	
March 31	5.50	
May 19	5.50	
July 1	5.50	
August 18	5.50	
September 29	5.25	
October 15	5.00	
November 17	4.75	
December 22	4.75	
Start of 1999	4.75	
February 3	4.75	
March 30	4.75	
May 18	4.75	
June 30	5.00	
August 24	5.25	
October 5	5.25	
November 16	5.50	
December 21	5.50	
Start of 2000	5.50	Neutral
February 2	5.75	Inflation
March 21	6.00	Inflation
May 16	6.50	Inflation
June 28	6.50	Inflation
August 22	6.50	Inflation
October 3	6.50	Inflation
November 15	—	—
December 19	—	—

funds target rate—its bank rate in Wicksell's terms. Fearing inflation, it will raise it. Fearing economic stagnation, it will lower it.
Most of the time, it does nothing. In recent years, this activity
seems to have given rise to a misunderstanding that can have per-
nicious implications.

Perhaps, having pored over the most recent data, the Fed will
decide at one of its FOMC meetings that it isn't yet time to reset its
fed funds target rate, but it is time to be concerned about inflation
and watchful for signs of unhealthy growth in the factors that
cause inflation. Following the meeting, the FOMC will issue a
statement of its bias, or its assessment of the preponderance of
risks—toward inflation or recession. If the bias is toward inflation,
the expectation is that the next interest-rate move will be up.

The logic of this is simple: Inflation occurs when too much
money chases too few goods. The higher the cost of credit, the less
credit consumers and businesses will demand. The less credit, the
less spending. Ultimately, then, cutting off or at least curtailing the
supply of credit should rein in inflation.

Of course, investors always try to get ahead of the curve. On
hearing what the Fed has to say, the denizens of the financial markets will heed the warning. Portfolio managers for large pension
funds, poised to buy Treasury securities or corporate bonds, may
reason that if inflation is a threat, they need to get more return for
taking the investment risk. If very much of this goes on, interest
rates will start edging up, even before the Fed acts.

For the last few years, whenever this happens, it has become
fashionable to say that the market is doing the Fed's work for it.
Some among the pundits have even gone so far as to say that this
responsiveness of the market has rendered the Fed irrelevant. This
is simply wrong.

The Fed Is Irrelevant?
Guess Again

Think of the power the Fed has. It has the power to create credit
and money, figuratively, out of thin air. The Fed has been granted
the state monopoly to produce counterfeit money. What is unique
about this is that when the Fed creates more credit, or "prints"
more money, spending in the economy unambiguously increases.

We cannot say that spending increases unambiguously if you or we grant more credit. Why? Because we cannot print money—legally, at least. The way we typically grant more credit is by saving more. Saving more means spending less. So, when we grant more credit, we transfer some of our spending to the borrower, as in the case of the Bozo scheme. His spending rises. Ours falls by the same amount. As a result, for the economy as a whole, net spending does not change.

Getting back to Greenspan & Co., the Fed sets an interest rate at which it is willing to supply all the credit demanded. Suppose that the private sector's demand for credit were to rise. This would start to put upward pressure on interest rates. But, because the Fed is targeting an interest rate, it prints up some new money with which to purchase government securities. It keeps printing and purchasing until it gets the interest rate back down to the target level. By purchasing government debt with its freshly minted money, the Fed is creating credit. Although it is not directly accommodating the private sector's increased demand for credit—not lending directly to the bozos of the world—the Fed is doing so indirectly. By purchasing government debt, it is providing the sellers of that government debt with money with which to purchase private-sector debt. The private-sector borrower increases his or her spending with the proceeds of his or her new loan, and no one else in the economy need cut back on his or her spending.

Now, suppose that the Fed decides to raise the interest rate at which it is willing to create money and credit to all comers. How does it effect the rate rise? By selling government securities from its portfolio. This means that the Fed is reducing the amount of credit it is willing to supply to the economy. Another way of looking at this would be to say that the Fed's demand for credit has risen—it wants to exchange a government IOU for the public's money. The Fed keeps selling government securities to the public until the interest rate rises to the Fed's new target level. Where does the public get the money with which to purchase securities from the Fed? Either by selling other securities that it owns (perhaps private-sector ones), by cutting back on its current spending (perhaps saving more), or most likely, by some combination of the two. The sale of private-sector securities will put upward pressure on the private sector's cost of funds. This will curb spending. The act of saving will obviously reduce the spending of the savers.

The upshot of all this is that as long as there is some inverse sensitivity of private-sector credit demand with respect to the level of interest rates, the Fed can affect total spending in the economy by varying the amount of credit it creates for the economy. That is, to achieve its desired effect on spending, the Fed will have to change the amount of credit it supplies more or less depending on how sensitive private-sector borrowers are to interest-rate levels and on how much the demand for credit is changing.

Suppose the Fed wants to slow the pace of spending in the economy. It will have to reduce the amount of credit it provides by a greater amount if private-sector credit demand proves relatively insensitive to interest-rate levels than it would if private-sector demand proves relatively sensitive to changes in interest-rate levels.

The same is true with regard to the credit demand curve. As long as the demand for credit remains relatively constant, the Fed will have to do less than it would if the credit demand curve were shifting out at a faster rate.

These are the factors that determine how much the Fed has to raise interest rates in order to accomplish its goals, not whether banks have a larger or smaller share of the credit market relative to GSEs or other credit intermediaries. The market can anticipate a Fed policy shift all it wants. Ultimately, the Fed still must take action.

Two Basic Ideas

Think for a minute about the terms *economic growth* and *inflation*. You hear them used without good understanding too much of the time. They're really areas on a scale rather than different economic states. But they're not really hard ideas at bottom.

This description of economic growth oversimplifies and abstracts away from lots of detail, but the basic idea is that if people have good jobs and incomes, they'll want more and better houses, cars, clothes—all kinds of things. Ideally, this greater demand should lead to increases in production capacity and increased employment. You often hear talk about creating new jobs. As long as the wants of consumers and the production capacity of the business sector remain more or less in sync, the economy will grow without inflation. At least, the rate of inflation growth won't be enough to be damaging. If demand exceeds supply, you get inflation. If supply exceeds demand, you get recession. The Fed's goal is to find the balancing point.

Economists often describe inflation as a condition that occurs when too many dollars are chasing too few goods. You might read in a financial paper, such as the *Wall Street Journal*, that the Fed has expressed concern about a given group of labor settlements, for example. Here's why. Suppose that several corporations give their workers 8 percent raises, but productivity and production capacity stay the same. In such a case, a huge number of people will have more money, but the number of cars, refrigerators, TVs, and so on that are available for sale stays the same. These people will pay more to buy the same things. If a $600 refrigerator suddenly becomes a $900 refrigerator, then a dollar is worth less because it buys less. This is why inflation is a problem. It erodes the value of money and everything else. When this happens, you might hear the workers who got the 8 percent raises complaining that they're making more than ever and feeling poorer. They are probably right.

If the Fed plays its cards right, the economy can avoid this situation. If the corporations can manage to pay their workers a little less and put the rest of that money into new productive capacity—new facilities, more efficient technology, whatever—then at the same time people have more to spend and there's more to spend it on. When this happens, the economy grows in a noninflationary way, and everybody is better off.

Transfer Credit and Created Credit

When it comes to understanding the roles of consumers, financial intermediaries (such as banks, GSEs, and other nonbank financial institutions), it is crucial to distinguish between *transfer credit* and *created credit* and how they affect the structure of interest rates and the spending power of the economy at large. This discussion and the accompanying exhibits abstract away from many details, but they should make clear what a finite supply of credit can do to the structure of interest rates and how such a situation contrasts with one where the supply of credit is open-ended.

The diagram labeled "State 1" (Exhibit 2-2*a*) assumes a finite money supply and an economy with two potential consumers. Consumer 1 has no disposable income. Consumer 2 has $1,500 of disposable income. Both have things they want—TVs, camping equipment, a computer—each want having the same price tag for the sake of discussion. You can see that with the economy in State 1, Consumer 2 can satisfy all three of her wants, but Consumer 1 cannot satisfy his wants.

The diagram labeled "State 2" (Exhibit 2-2*b*) starts from the same assumptions and includes the same two consumers, each with the same wants. In this case, Consumer 1 asks Consumer 2 to lend him enough money to satisfy his want in exchange for which he will pay an amount of interest, *r*, they both agree is fair at a certain time. Now Consumer 1 can satisfy his need, but notice that Consumer 2 had to postpone satisfying one of her needs. The circle-slash symbol signifies this difference between State 1 and State 2. Of course, as the label on the dashed repayment line indicates, Consumer 2 gets $500 plus *r* to repay her for the postponement.

Notice that the process of State 2 does not increase the spending power of the economy. It simply transfers part of Consumer 2's spending power to Consumer 1. Also, consider the fact that this kind of activity will ultimately exert upward pressure on interest rates.

Exhibit 2-2a State 1

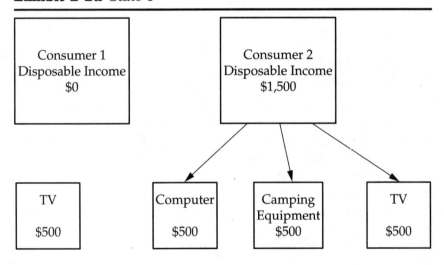

Exhibit 2-2b State 2

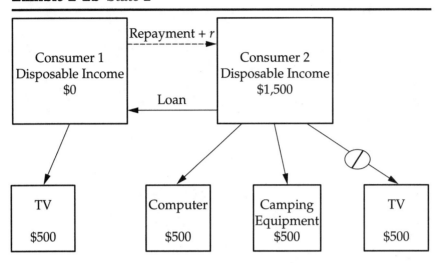

The diagram labeled "State 3" (Exhibit 2-2c) introduces a significant change in the form of the oval labeled "Central Bank." To prevent unwanted upward pressure on interest rates, a central bank can create new credit (that is, it can print money). In the actual case, the central bank will not lend directly to Consumer 1. Rather, it will buy government securities from the handful of primary dealers with whom it does business directly. Details aside, notice what happens in this case. Consumer 2 can satisfy all three of her wants immediately, but Consumer 1 can satisfy his want as well. Importantly, the Central Bank's action in State 3 has increased the buying power of this little economy and removed the upward pressure on interest rates.

From time to time you hear it said that the banks or the nonbank financial firms such as GSEs are doing too much lending. The worry is that they will create an economically harmful situation by creating too much credit. The diagram labeled "State 4" (Exhibit 2-2d) addresses this worry and shows it to be unfounded. State 4 returns to the assumptions of State 1. The supply of money is finite, and the economy contains two consumers who, between them, want the same four things. What is different here is the presence of a financial intermediary.

In this version of the world, Consumer 2 might still decide it is worth it to postpone buying the TV (again note the circle-slash to

Exhibit 2-2c State 3

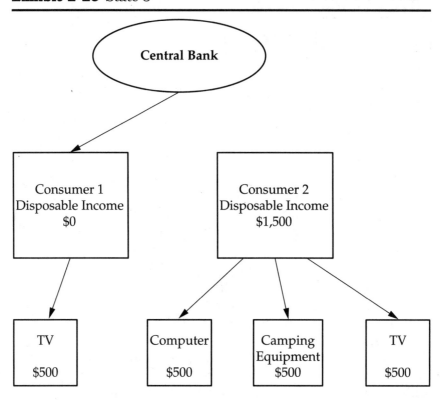

indicate that the purchase wasn't made), but this time she will invest in the intermediary to earn the promised rate of return, r, instead of loaning the money directly to Consumer 1. Having gotten this money from Consumer 2, the intermediary can lend it to Consumer 1. Naturally, the intermediary wants to make a profit for performing this service and so must charge Consumer 1 more than it has promised to pay Consumer 2—call it $r+$.

The economy represented in State 4, notice, has exactly the same spending power as the ones in States 1 and 2. Consumer 2 must still prefer to postpone some of her spending for the opportunity to earn r in order for the intermediary to be able to make a loan to Consumer 1 and earn $r+$. Importantly, the intermediary is only a conduit for this set of transactions. Although it does charge a fee for its service, the intermediary does not do anything here that increases the buying power of the economy. As is the case in State 2, the credit

Exhibit 2-2d State 4

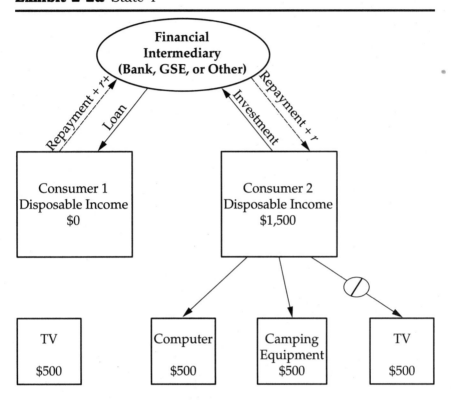

extended here is transfer credit because it transfers some of Consumer 2's buying power to Consumer 1. You can see how this will exert even more upward pressure on interest rates than the situation in State 2.

The diagram labeled "State 5" (Exhibit 2-2e) brings all this together. Here, the Central Bank again creates more credit. This won't go directly to the intermediary any more than it will go directly to Consumer 1 in State 3—unless the intermediary happens to be one of the primary dealers. In State 5, the intermediary still serves as no more than a conduit, but again the buying power of the economy increases by enough to allow both consumers to satisfy their wants immediately and to overcome upward pressure on interest rates. Here, as in State 3, the Central Bank has created new credit. As far as the creation of credit is concerned, the presence of the intermediary remains irrelevant.

Exhibit 2-2e State 5

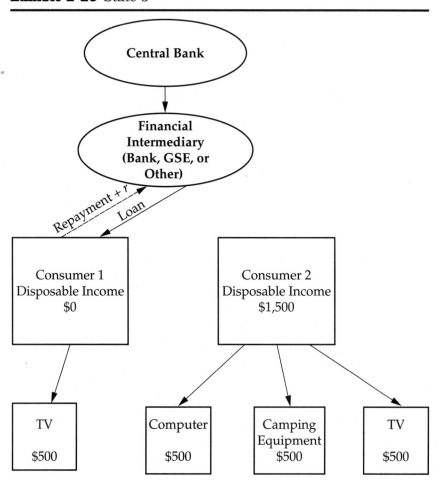

3

Fed Funds Spreads Can Shed Light on Future Fed Actions

Perhaps no single interest rate is watched more carefully than the fed funds target rate set by the Federal Open Market Committee (FOMC or, popularly, the Fed). Perhaps, too, no single financial policy decision carries more weight in all corners of the financial world than FOMC decisions concerning whether to raise, lower, or leave untouched the fed funds target.

In media reports, "a Fed meeting" is shorthand for "a meeting of the Federal Open Market Committee (FOMC)." The voting members of this group consist of the governors of the Federal Reserve, the president of the Federal Reserve Bank of New York, and a subset of the other Fed bank presidents on a rotating basis, although all of them sit in on the meetings. Its special charge is to consider whether, in light of all known factors, to adjust the fed funds target rate and the discount rate. The goal, always, is to sustain growth and head off inflation before it grows enough to hurt the economy.

The reasons for this are not hard to find. This is the one interest rate the U.S. Federal Reserve can actually control. A policy change with regard to this interest rate signals the Fed consensus concerning economic growth and inflation. This number, more than any other single number, distills the deliberations of Fed leaders and their staffs about the health of the U.S. economy. If they fear that impending inflation will ravage the spending power of consumers, they raise the target, or tighten. If they sense that economic growth is slowing to a worrisome degree, they lower the target, or ease. If they sense that the economy is percolating along at an acceptable rate, they leave well enough alone.

Importantly, these policy decisions show up in the economy with a 5- or 6-month lag. As a result, a Fed move serves as a useful early signal of what may emerge that far in the future.

Through close monitoring of the Chicago Board of Trade 30-day fed funds futures, thoughtful investors can anticipate Fed policy shifts in a useful way. So it will be well worth your while to see how these futures work and learn how you can extract the useful information these data contain.

Defining Fed Funds Futures

The 30-day fed funds futures contract calls for delivery of the interest rate paid on $5 million of overnight fed funds held for 30 days. The contract is cash settled against the monthly average of the daily fed funds effective rate, calculated and reported each business day by the Federal Reserve Bank of New York, for the delivery month. This monthly average calculation uses the actual number of calendar days in the month, including weekends and holidays. The exchange lists futures contracts for the current calendar month and the succeeding 24 months, although active trading typically occurs only in the first 5 or 6 months listed.

The futures price for the front, or delivery, month amounts to 100 minus the monthly average fed funds rate. For example, a monthly average fed funds rate of 6.52 percent implies a futures price of 93.48 (100 − 6.52 = 93.48). Conversely, a futures price of 93.52 implies a fed funds rate of 6.48 percent (100 − 93.52 = 6.48 percent).

Back-month prices—that is, prices for any but the current month—result from market activity in the context of the current yield curve. If the interest-rate outlook is stable, the interest rate for each succeeding month should be between 3 and 4 basis points higher than the current rate simply because of compounding effect. The typical bid-ask spread in the cash fed funds market is about 3 basis points. Putting these two factors together, you might see month-to-month spreads of anywhere from 4 to 9 basis points in an equilibrium market.

Although only banks that are members of the Federal Reserve System can trade in the cash fed funds market, the market for fed funds futures contracts is open to anyone with an opinion about how this all-important interest rate might change in the near future. As with all futures markets, this one distills information from many sources into a set of publicly traded, and therefore remarkably transparent, prices. These prices amount to a consensus view that, in the aggregate, will incorporate more information than is available to any one forecaster or "expert." The public and open nature of these markets allows them to process new information immediately.

For example, as new inflation data emerge, fed funds futures prices will reflect the shift in market outlook well before more conventional sources have processed the new information. Similarly, when the Fed chairman gives testimony to Congress or makes a speech that signals a new leaning on the part of the Fed, the futures market will incorporate this into its bids and offers in minutes, and price screens around the world will reflect this new consensus.

Deriving the Market Consensus

A simple exercise can help you interpret the market consensus implicit in the fed funds futures data any time this kind of information will be helpful to your investment decision making. A convenient source of price information is the futures page of the third section of the daily *Wall Street Journal*, but the same information is available from various quote vendors and from the Chicago Board of Trade (CBOT) Web site (*www.cbot.com*). (See Exhibit 3-1a and b for examples of the *Wall Street Journal* and CBOT quotation formats.)

- Using the *Wall Street Journal* futures quotes, first find the prices under the heading "Settle." Using CBOT quotes, locate the prices in the "Last 1" row. Note the prices for the first five contracts listed (generally, the first 5 months show trading activity, as Exhibit 3-2 shows). On September 22, 2000, these were the September, October, November, December, and January contracts.

Exhibit 3-1a Example of the *Wall Street Journal* Quotation Format

INTEREST RATE

	OPEN	HIGH	LOW	SETTLE	CHANGE	LIFETIME HIGH	LIFETIME LOW	OPEN INT.
Treasury Bonds (CBT)-$100,000; pts 32nds of 100%								
Sept	97-27	98-09	97-27	98-04	+ 7	101-00	88-19	16,913
Dec	97-29	98-08	97-25	98-03	+ 7	101-02	88-31	387,809
Mr01	98-04	98-05	97-27	98-01	+ 6	100-30	1	1,432
Est vol 200,000; vol Mon 294,290; open int 406,295, −12,164.								
Treasury Bonds (MCE)-$50,000; pts 32nds of 100%								
Sept	98-04	98-08	97-31	98-04	+ 5	100-31	92-23	10
Dec	98-03	98-08	97-27	98-03	+ 5	101-02	95-06	1,605
Est vol 500; vol Mon 767; open int 1,616, −117.								
Treasury Notes (CBT)-$100,000; pts 32nds of 100%								
Sept	99-26	100-00	99-245	99-295	+ 3.0	100-23	94-22	23,201
Dec	99-22	99-26	99-18	99-235	+ 3.0	00-205	96-075	507,523
Mr01	99-245	99-265	99-235	99-265	+ 2.5	00-195	98-04	800
Est vol 151,000; vol Mon 210,411; open int 531,524, −12,331.								
10 Yr Agency Notes (CBT)-$100,000; pts 32nds of 100%								
Sept	93-28	94-005	93-275	93-285	− 2.0	94-19	88-045	9,019
Dec	93-30	93-30	93-23	93-245	− 2.0	94-18	91-17	42,562
Est vol 7,100; vol Mon 8,774; open int 51,581. −1,013.								
5 Yr Treasury Notes (CBT)-$100,000; pts 32nds of 100%								
Sept	100-12	100-12	100-05	00-065	− 1.5	100-12	96-14	3,400
Dec	100-12	00-165	00-055	100-11	− 1.5	100-18	98-13	364,601
Est vol 73,000; vol Mon 72,434; open int 368,008, −12,844.								
2 Yr Treasury Notes (CBT)-$200,000; pts 32nds of 100%								
Sept	99-28	99-295	99-27	99-28	− 2.2	99-31	98-025	1,750
Dec	100-02	00-025	99-295	100-00	− 1.2	00-025	99-12	42,873
Est vol 2,400; vol Mon 7,036; open int 44,423, −3,084.								
30 Day Federal Funds (CBT)-$5 million; pts of 100%								
Sept	93.480	93.485	93.480	93.480	+ .005	93.640	93.350	12,352
Oct	93.51	93.51	93.51	93.51	....	93.52	92.93	12,985
Nov	93.52	93.52	93.50	93.51	− .01	93.52	92.90	13,214
Dec	93.52	93.53	93.50	93.51	− .01	93.53	93.11	14,436
Ja01	93.52	93.54	93.51	93.52	....	93.54	93.25	1,149
Feb	93.57	93.58	93.56	93.57	− .01	93.58	92.59	824
Est vol 4,500; vol Mon 8,364; open int 55,739, +1,011.								
Muni Bond Index (CBT)-$1,000; times Bond Buyer MBI								
Sept	99-00	99-07	99-00	99.07	+ 6	100-16	90-03	6,654
Dec	98-03	98-09	98-01	98-08	+ 6	99-24	91-19	16,422
Est vol 5,000; vol Mon 1,849; open int 23,076, +174.								
Index Close 98-26; Yield 5.86.								
Treasury Bills (CME)-$1 mil.; pts of 100%								

Exhibit 3-1b Example of the Chicago Board of Trade (CBOT)
Quotation Format

September 22, 2000 09:40 AM CDT — Open Outcry

30 Day Federal Funds

	00Sept	00Oct	00Nov	00Dec	01Jan	01Feb	01Mar	01Apr
Opening	93480	93520	93525	93550	93540	93575	93590	
	7:28 am	7:32 am	7:56 am	7:20 am	8:50 am	7:24 am	7:44 am	
High	93480	93520	93525	93550	93545	93590	93595	
	7:28 am	7:32 am	7:56 am	7:20 am	9:27 am	7:24 am	9:30 am	
Low	93480	93515	93515	93525	93540	93575	93590	
	7:28 am	7:40 am	8:56 am	8:45 am	8:50 am	7:24 am	7:44 am	
Last 3		93515	93520	93525		93580		
		7:40 am	8:25 am	8:45 am		8:45 am		
Last 2		93520	93515	93530	93540	93585	93590	93600
		7:41 am	8:56 am	9:26 am	8:50 am	9:30 am	7:44 am	7:28 am
Last 1	93480	93515	93515	93530	93545	93585	93595	93700
	7:28 am	8:43 am	9:25 am	9:34 am	9:27 am	9:38 am	9:30 am	7:28 am
Net Chg	Unch	+5	+10	+20	+20	+30	+30	Unch
Prev Setl	93480	93510	93505	93510	93525	93555	93565	93590
High Limits								
Low Limits								
	00Sept	00Oct	00Nov	00Dec	01Jan	01Feb	01Mar	01Apr

SOURCE : Chicago Board of Trade

Exhibit 3-2 Tracking Fed Funds
Trading Activity

	Volume in contracts traded		
	9/15/00	9/20/00	9/22/00
Sep	21	765	1,089
Oct	4,843	1,292	2,351
Nov	1,466	971	1,179
Dec	2,581	1,140	1,062
Jan	114	91	246
Feb	63	184	71
Mar	142	26	1
Apr	2	0	0

DATA SOURCE : Chicago Board of Trade

Exhibit 3-3 Calculating Fed Funds Spreads (CBOT Quotes)

Futures contract	Futures price	Implied rate	Monthly spreads
Sep	93.48	6.52	—
Oct	93.52	6.48	−0.04
Nov	93.52	6.48	0.00
Dec	93.53	6.47	−0.01
Jan	93.55	6.45	−0.02

DATA SOURCE: Chicago Board of Trade

- Find the interest rate each price implies by subtracting the price from 100, and rounding up to a whole basis point.

- Determine the month-to-month interest-rate spreads by subtracting the September rate from the October rate (for example, using Exhibit 3-3 data: 6.48 − 6.52 = −0.04), the October rate from the November rate, and so on.

Exhibit 3-3 illustrates the results of this calculation, based on September 22, 2000 prices.

Note that these fed funds rates are percentages. In decimal terms, 6.52 is equivalent to 0.0652. Also, in financial market usage, a *basis point* is one one-hundredth of a percentage point, or 0.0001. Accordingly, a 0.04 September-October spread represents a 4-basis-point difference, or 0.0004 in decimal terms.

With the next FOMC meetings scheduled for October 3, 2000 and November 15, 2000, these flat spreads indicate that the market expected no Fed policy shift at either meeting.

Tracking a Shifting Consensus

Although market watchers tend to focus on absolute prices or interest-rate levels, absolute levels often carry less information than relationships among contract months, or spreads. Certainly this is true in the fed funds markets.

Given that equilibrium or normality implies spreads of 4 to 9 basis points between contract months, a gap or jump in the spreads will signal that the market expects a Fed move. Negative spreads suggest a consensus toward easing. Positive spreads signal the anticipation of a tightening.

A look at history shows how this can work. Exhibit 3-4 illustrates the spreads for three days during October and November 1998. In 1998, the FOMC had lowered its target at its September 29 meeting from 5.50 to 5.25 percent.

During this period, recall, the market was coping with the fallout from the Russian credit debacle and the Long-Term Capital Management crisis and was anticipating FOMC meetings scheduled for November 17, 1998 and December 22, 1998. The 17-basis-point November-December spread in the October 1 array departs strongly from the 4 to 9 basis points of an equilibrium situation. This suggests that the market expected another 25-basis-point easing at the November meeting. Notice that the shift shows up in the pricing of the contract for December, not November. Because the fed funds effective rate is averaged to determine the futures price for

Exhibit 3-4 Comparing Market Readings

Futures contract	Futures price	Implied rate	Monthly spreads
October 1, 1998			
Dec	95.06	4.94	−0.17
Jan	95.18	4.82	−0.12
Feb	95.39	4.61	−0.21
October 20, 1998			
Oct	94.93	5.07	—
Nov	95.09	4.91	−0.16
Dec	95.27	4.73	−0.18
Jan	95.36	4.64	−0.09
Feb	95.67	4.33	−0.31
November 5, 1998			
Nov	95.06	4.94	—
Dec	95.14	4.86	−0.08
Jan	95.20	4.80	−0.06
Feb	95.45	4.55	−0.25
Mar	95.44	4.56	0.01

DATA SOURCE: Chicago Board of Trade

the delivery month, a late-month shift will not have much impact on that month's price. As a result, changes anticipated at a meeting falling late in the month will be reflected in the pricing of the following month's futures—in this case, in the December futures contract.

The Fed surprised virtually everyone with a move on October 15. This was surprising because policy shifts rarely occur outside regularly scheduled meetings. Shortly after, the market began altering its expectations. The October 20 spreads reflect a continued leaning toward further easing at the November meeting, but notice the 31-basis-point January-February spread. This indicates that the market saw a somewhat higher probability that the move would occur at the February 3, 1999 meeting. Note that with a meeting scheduled for this early in February, the February price will reflect the anticipated policy shift.

By early November, the February preference had solidified. The market no longer seemed to be considering the possibility of a November move. Its money was on a February easing, as the more normal 8-basis-point November-December spread and the 6-basis-point December-January spread show. The market held to this expectation of a February ease until the December FOMC meeting. After that, the spreads remained relatively flat through the end of February, and indeed, there was no policy shift until the June 30, 1999 FOMC meeting, when the Fed raised the target back up to 5 percent.

Shifting from a Stable Outlook to Expectations of Tightening

In early June 2000, you might have seen spreads like the ones in Exhibit 3-5.

Exhibit 3-5 A Typical Fed Funds Futures Array

Futures contract	Futures price	Implied rate	Monthly spreads
Jun	93.48	6.52	—
Jul	93.40	6.60	0.08
Aug	93.33	6.67	0.07
Sep	93.25	6.75	0.08
Oct	92.20	6.80	0.05

DATA SOURCE: Chicago Board of Trade

The next Fed meetings were to be held June 28, August 22, and October 3. These spreads all range between 4 and 9 basis points—well within normal limits. They signal that the market anticipated no Fed action at any of these three meetings.

On the day of the June meeting, however, the market took a different view of the situation, as Exhibit 3-6 shows.

The 14-basis-point August-September spread seems out of line with the others. What has happened here is that the market (all the people who are using fed funds futures to hedge or to take positions on what they think the Fed will do at its August 22 meeting) has decided that the Fed will probably hike its fed funds target from 6.50 to 6.75 percent.

Note carefully: It is not the 6.74 percent implied fed funds rate of the September contract that sends this signal but the dislocation in the spreads. Market activity will often result in an implied yield rather far from the new target. Here, the fact that the number is right on target is mere coincidence. Yet the spread will still reflect what the market expects. You must simply focus on the dislocation in the spreads rather than on the levels of the implied rates. Of course, the economic news of the next day or week can change this. Then the spreads will reflect the new expectations of the market.

In this case, economic data continued to issue forth, and only 9 days later the market was changing its collective mind. Any idea of an August 22 target shift was completely gone by August 3, as the flat and narrow spreads of Exhibit 3-7 show.

At times, these spreads can reflect remarkably strong views, and they respond quickly to shifts in the market consensus as thousands of people, each with his or her own expertise and context for evaluating, sift through the constantly emerging economic data.

Exhibit 3-6 An Altered Market Consensus

Futures contract	Futures price	Implied rate	Monthly spreads
Jun	93.48	6.52	—
Jul	93.45	6.55	0.03
Aug	93.40	6.60	0.05
Sep	93.26	6.74	0.14
Oct	92.21	6.79	0.05

DATA SOURCE: Chicago Board of Trade

Exhibit 3-7 The Market Shifts Away from an August Move

Futures contract	Futures price	Implied rate	Monthly spreads
Aug	93.49	6.51	—
Sep	93.44	6.56	0.05
Oct	93.42	6.58	0.02
Nov	93.38	6.62	0.04
Dec	93.34	6.66	0.04

DATA SOURCE: Chicago Board of Trade

Tracking a Growing Consensus

Two Fed meetings that were anticipated with special concern were the February 2 and March 21, 2000 sessions. The fed funds futures spreads provide an interesting record of the growth of the market consensus during the period leading up to these meetings. Recall that in late December 1999 the fed funds target was 5.50 percent, and inflationary pressures were building in many sectors of the U.S. economy.

The crucial spread, relative to the February 2, 2000 FOMC meeting, was the January-February spread. Three months before the meeting, this spread suggested nothing about an impending Fed move. On October 6, 1999, the January-February spread was trading at 5 basis points. By October 19, this spread had widened to 14 basis points, a clear sign that the market anticipated action at the February meeting. Early in November, the economic news was such that the market allowed this spread to drop back to 9 basis points, but by the first of December it was back out to 15 basis points.

Remarkably, it exploded to 36 basis points on December 29 and ranged between 32 and 40 basis points right up until the February meeting. The economic reports at year-end gave rise to talk that the Fed might decide to raise the target 50 basis points at the February meeting, not the more usual 25 basis points. This talk continued all through January. When the smoke cleared on February 2, the Fed raised the target only 25 basis points—from 5.50 to 5.57 percent.

Already in early December, had you been tracking these fed funds futures spreads, you could have seen signs that the market expected another tightening at the March 21 FOMC meeting. Specifically, on December 2, you would have seen the spreads of Exhibit 3-8.

Exhibit 3-8 Anticipating Another Move in March

Futures contract	Futures price	Implied rate	Monthly spreads
Dec	94.53	5.47	—
Jan	94.50	5.50	0.03
Feb	94.33	5.68	0.18
Mar	94.28	5.72	0.05
Apr	94.19	5.81	0.09

DATA SOURCE: Chicago Board of Trade

Recall that because the front-month futures price (here, the December contract is the front month, but by the time of the March Fed meeting, it would be the March contract) is an average of the fed effective rate, a policy shift at a late-month meeting will have little effect on that month's price. Because of this, market users place their hedges or take positions on the following contract. As a result, the expectation of a policy shift at the March 21 meeting will show up as a shift in the relationship between the March and April contracts. This is why, thinking about what the Fed might do March 21, the market focus was on the March-April spread.

The signal on December 2 was far less strong than the January-February signal, but 9 basis points is still a noticeable dislocation from the 5-basis-point February-March spread. While this 9-basis-point spread lies at the upper end of normalcy, the change is enough to prompt a careful observer to begin keeping an eye on this spread.

By late December, the March-April spread had widened slightly to 11 basis points. Through most of January it hovered between 11 and 13 basis points—a sign that the market leaned toward a further hike in the fed funds target rate at the March meeting but wasn't totally convinced.

In late January, though, the market began to show signs that it was totally convinced. The January 28 March-April spread reading was 14 basis points. It crept up to 15 basis points and then on February 2, the day the FOMC raised the target to 5.75 percent, the March-April spread jumped to 19 basis points. The spread jumped briefly to 22 basis points but then settled back into a range between 17 and 19 basis points for the rest of February and March. This seemed to indicate that the market was convinced that the Fed would move the target another 25 basis points at its March meeting.

Finding the Probability of a Fed Policy Shift

In the weeks immediately prior to a Fed meeting, you may hear commentators say that fed funds futures prices suggest, for example, an 83 percent probability for a 50-basis-point boost in the fed funds target rate. These commentators are working from simple probability math, and you can do the same thing. Consider the market situation on August 3, 2000 (see Exhibit 3-7). Where the market had been expecting the Fed to raise its fed funds target from 6.50 to 6.75 percent, new data caused the market to change its view. Now it expected no change.

On August 3, the August fed funds futures contract settled at a price of 93.49, which implied a fed funds rate of 6.51 percent. Using a standard probability equation, you could have used this implied rate to estimate the probability that the Fed would either raise the target to 6.75 percent on August 22 or leave it unchanged at 6.50 percent:

$$6.50\% \times (22/31) + [6.75\%p + 6.50\%(1 - p)] \times (9/31) = 6.51\%$$

Here p is the probability that the Fed will tighten 25 basis points, $(1 - p)$ is the probability that the Fed will leave the target unchanged, 22/31 is the fraction of the month during which the target is known to be 6.50 percent, and 9/31 is the fraction of the month during which the target is unknown.

Solving for p, you will find that, in this case, $p = 0.1364$. That is, this exercise predicts a 14 percent probability that the Fed will raise its target rate 25 basis points and an 86 percent probability that it will leave the target unchanged.

In case algebra was a long time ago, here is the step-by-step process for solving for p. First, convert 22/31 and 9/31 into decimal fractions by dividing 22 by 31 and 9 by 31 to get 0.7097 and 0.2903. Next, rearrange the term $6.50(1 - p)$ into $-6.5\%p + 6.5\%$. These two steps result in this array:

$$6.50\% \times 0.7097 + (6.75\%p - 6.50\%p + 6.50\%) \times 0.2903 = 6.51\%$$

Now multiply 6.5 by 0.7097 and the three terms inside the parentheses by 0.2903 to produce this array:

$$4.6131 + 1.9595p - 1.8870p + 1.8870 = 6.51$$

Move the 4.6131 and 1.8870 to the other side of the equals sign by changing their signs to produce this:

$$1.9595p - 1.8870p = 6.51 - 4.6131 - 1.8870$$

Do the subtraction to produce this:

$$0.0726p = 0.0099$$

Shift the 0.0726 to the other side of the equals sign by dividing through to produce this:

$$p = 0.0099/0.0726$$

Do the division, and you can see that $p = 0.1364$, or a 14 percent probability.

These probability predictions should carry an important caveat that is too often observed in the breach. This equation assumes that the Fed has a two-choice menu. It can either shift the target the amount in question or leave the target unchanged. The Fed obviously works from a far richer menu. Suppose the consensus is that the Fed will tighten 50 basis points. The Fed can do this, but it can also surprise the market with 75- or 25-basis-point moves, do nothing, or even ease some amount. Adding even one more option to the menu requires a far more complicated set of calculations that are simply beyond most of us. As long as you recognize this limitation, though, this probability estimate can enrich your reading of the market estimate.

A Valuable Tool

When you observe the fluctuations in the fed funds spreads that have been pointed out during the course of this discussion, or when you note the shifts in the probability values you can derive from the implied fed funds rates, it is easy to conclude that these markets are rather error prone. This would be a mistake. Consider that all these readings reflect what the market knows on a given day and what it *anticipates* given that knowledge. The next day, or week, the market may well have different information to process and thus may "know" something else.

The point is that fed funds futures—and indeed, futures markets in general—provide a means for you to track this ever-shifting consensus as it unfolds rather than after the fact, as with so much economic data. This makes these futures a valuable tool for financial decision makers apart from their value as trading and risk-management tools.

4

Yield-Curve Shape Changes Foretell Economic Developments

You've seen that attention to the fed funds futures spreads can help you anticipate shifts in Federal Reserve (Fed) policy and so help you tune in on what the market thinks the Fed thinks about the economy. Another market-based forecasting tool is the U.S. Treasury yield curve, although few investors seem to have more than a cursory grasp of what the curve has to "say" to them.

A *yield curve* simply plots the yields of fixed-income securities at key maturities. The most commonly cited yield curve is the U.S. Treasury yield curve, two versions of which are shown in Exhibit 4-1. Time was when you could probably learn all you needed to know from a study of the U.S. Treasury yield curve. Currently, though, it seems important to consider sovereign debt curves such as the ones for Germany and Japan and yield curves showing the relationships among corporate debt issuance at various credit ratings.

You can see that the two curves in Exhibit 4-1 connect the yields of the most recently issued U.S. Treasury securities at the 3- and 6-month and 1-, 2-, 5-, 10-, and 30-year maturities as of November 18, 1999 and 9 months later on August 18, 2000.

The November 18 curve represents what analysts call a normal yield curve. Here, the longer the maturity, the higher the yield, and this results in an upward-sloping curve. The August 18 curve

Exhibit 4-1 Treasury Yield Curves, November 18, 1999 and August 18, 2000

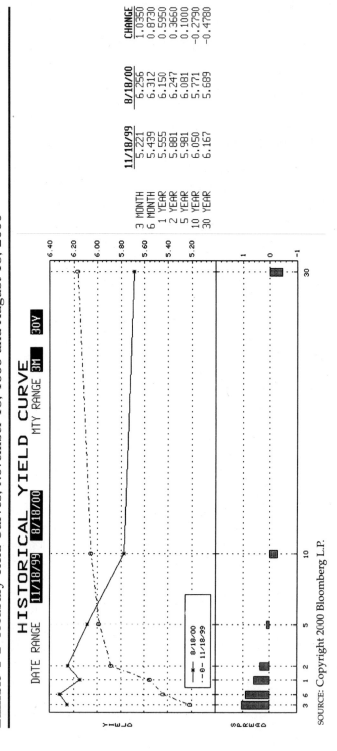

HISTORICAL YIELD CURVE

DATE RANGE 11/18/99   8/18/00   MTY RANGE 3M   30Y

	11/18/99	8/18/00	CHANGE
3 MONTH	5.221	6.256	1.0350
6 MONTH	5.439	6.312	0.8730
1 YEAR	5.555	6.150	0.5950
2 YEAR	5.881	6.247	0.3660
5 YEAR	5.981	6.081	0.1000
10 YEAR	6.050	5.771	-0.2790
30 YEAR	6.167	5.689	-0.4780

— * — 8/18/00
--- o --- 11/18/99

SOURCE: Copyright 2000 Bloomberg L.P.

illustrates a downward-sloping, or inverted, yield curve. In this case, the longer the maturity, the lower the yield. Similar yield-curve pictures are shown on a daily basis in financial newspapers and on screen-based quotation sources.

Flatter-Steeper

Even normal yield curves differ in shape, and such changes can give helpful signals. Contrast the September 20, 1999 and November 18, 1999 yield curves shown in Exhibit 4-2. You can tell, just by looking, that the November curve is flatter than the September one.

Yield-curve analysts measure steepness or flatness in terms of the difference between two yields, most often the shortest and the longest. In this case, consider that the September spread between the 3-month and 10-year yields was 123 basis points. Two months later that spread was only 83 basis points. The November curve, then, was 40 basis points flatter than the September curve.

Investors often focus on a curve segment rather than on the whole curve. They may be concerned primarily with the 2- and 10-year yields. Exhibit 4-2 shows that part of the yield curve to have flattened as well. In September, the 2- to 10-year spread was 26 basis points. By November 18, it had flattened 9 basis points to 17 basis points.

Yield Curves As Indicators

Conventional wisdom holds that a normal yield curve signals a growing, healthy economy, while an inverted yield curve signals an approaching recession—or at least slower economic growth. This seems to be an oversimplification.

As an investor, you need to consider why the yield curve has one shape or another. You need to ask what happened during this period to cause the shape change you see. And you should probably consider yield curves other than the Treasury yield curve. Of course, what you want your yield-curve study to lead to is information about what might happen in the economy and how that can shape your investment decision making.

Exhibit 4-2 Treasury Yield Curves, September 20, 1999 and November 18, 1999

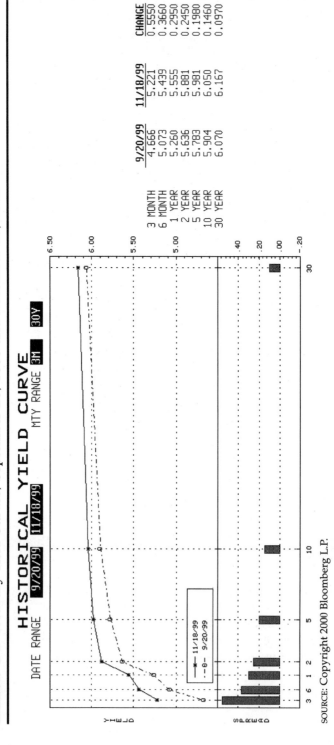

	9/20/99	11/18/99	CHANGE
3 MONTH	4.666	5.221	0.5550
6 MONTH	5.073	5.439	0.3660
1 YEAR	5.260	5.555	0.2950
2 YEAR	5.636	5.881	0.2450
5 YEAR	5.783	5.981	0.1980
10 YEAR	5.904	6.050	0.1460
30 YEAR	6.070	6.167	0.0970

HISTORICAL YIELD CURVE

DATE RANGE 9/20/99 11/18/99   MTY RANGE 3M   30Y

— ✳ — 11/18-99
- -□- - 9/20-99

Accounting for Yield-Curve Shape

In attempting to understand why the yield-curve shape is changing as it is, it is helpful to distinguish between the short and long ends of the curve. Generally, the short end of the curve includes the yields from 3 months to 2 years. The long end includes the coupon-paying securities from 3 out to 30 years. You often hear people question why, given recent Fed action, their mortgage rates aren't responding as these people expect them to. In fact, mortgages, being long-term propositions, respond to factors other than Fed action.

At the Short End, It's the Fed

In general, Fed policy seems the most important single factor to look at in attempting to explain the behavior of the short end of the yield curve. Further, market anticipation of Fed moves may be almost as important as the Fed moves themselves in some cases.

Notice the contrast between the 3-month to 2-year segments of the February 1, 1996 and August 1, 1996 Treasury yield curves shown in Exhibit 4-3. In February, the 2-year yield was actually 35 basis points lower than the 5.25 percent fed funds target, even after a 25-basis-point easing the day before brought the target down from 5.50 percent. Clearly, in February, interest-rate market participants anticipated further Fed easing, and that, more than anything else, probably accounted for the shape of that part of the yield curve. Of course, the Fed did nothing more through the spring and summer.

By the beginning of August, those same market participants just as clearly anticipated something quite different. The economic numbers during the past several months had convinced a majority of investment managers that the Fed would have to tighten soon. As a result, the 2-year yield worked up to a point 82 basis points over the fed funds rate, when it had been 35 basis points under it in February.

At the Long End, Inflation Concerns Reign

From the 5-year sector out to the 30-year sector, the story differs markedly. In February, the 30-year yield was 85 basis points over the 5-year yield. By early August, the spread had narrowed to 44 basis points. That segment of the yield curve had flattened considerably during those 6 months.

Exhibit 4-3 Treasury Yield Curves, February 1, 1996 and August 1, 1996

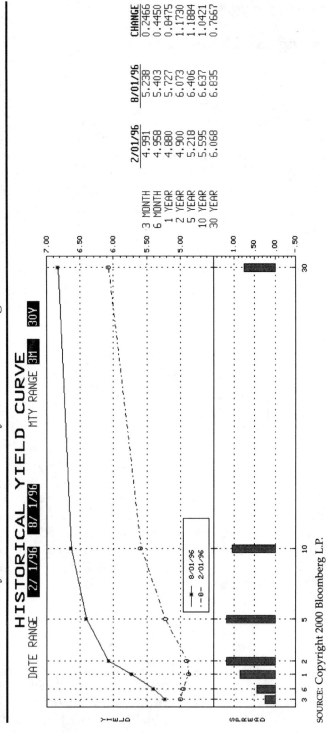

	2/01/96	8/01/96	CHANGE
3 MONTH	4.991	5.238	0.2466
6 MONTH	4.958	5.403	0.4450
1 YEAR	4.880	5.727	0.8475
2 YEAR	4.900	6.073	1.1730
5 YEAR	5.218	6.406	1.1884
10 YEAR	5.595	6.637	1.0421
30 YEAR	6.068	6.835	0.7667

HISTORICAL YIELD CURVE

DATE RANGE 2/ 1/96   8/ 1/96   MTY RANGE 3M   30Y

— * — 8/-01/96
-- ⊖ -- 2/-01/96

Just as the short end responds mainly to Fed policy, the long end responds mainly to inflation expectations. Logically enough, inflation worries investors in longer-maturity securities more than it does investors in shorter-maturity securities. The evidence of these two curves suggests that the long market is less concerned than it was. Perhaps it is possible to infer that the flattening of the long end amounts to a vote of confidence in the Fed as inflation fighter.

In February, when short-end investors were apparently expecting further easing, long-end investors were saying, in effect, "Wait a minute. Don't forget about the danger of inflation." By August, the short-end crowd was saying that the Fed would tighten soon, and the long-end crowd was saying that it had confidence that the Fed had things under control.

Complicating Our Understanding of Yield-Curve Shape

Expectations concerning Fed action and inflation fears are by no means separate issues. Indeed, these two yield-curve drivers often interact in complex and interesting ways.

Take 1994, for example. Starting that February, the Fed began a series of preemptive strikes against inflation. It boosted the fed funds target for several months in a row—several of the moves being 50-basis-point jolts, once even a 75-basis-point shot. By early 1995, the Fed had boosted the target 300 basis points.

Even though yields at all maturities continued to rise, yields at the longer maturities rose least. Exhibit 4-4 contrasts the February 2, 1994 and December 2, 1994 Treasury yield curves. You can see at a glance that while all yields rose in response to the Fed's action, the four shorter-term yields rose far more than the three longer-term yields. As a result, the December 2 curve is much flatter than the February 2 curve.

Subtracting 3-month yields from 30-year yields for the two 1994 dates, as has been done in Exhibit 4-5, you can see that while the February 2 curve was a steep 316 basis points, the December 2 curve was 212 basis points, 104 basis points flatter. (Note that a basis point is ¹⁄₁₀₀, or 0.01, of a percentage point. Accordingly, 3.16 percentage points is the same as 316 basis points.)

Exhibit 4-4 Treasury Yield Curves, February 2, 1994 and December 2, 1994

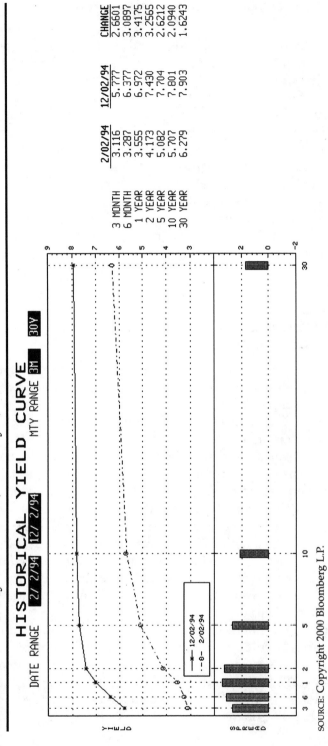

	2/02/94	12/02/94	CHANGE
3 MONTH	3.116	5.777	2.6601
6 MONTH	3.287	6.377	3.0897
1 YEAR	3.555	6.972	3.4175
2 YEAR	4.173	7.430	3.2565
5 YEAR	5.082	7.704	2.6212
10 YEAR	5.707	7.801	2.0940
30 YEAR	6.279	7.903	1.6243

SOURCE: Copyright 2000 Bloomberg L.P.

Exhibit 4-5 Contrasting 3-Month and
30-Year Yields

	30-year	3-month	Slope
February 2	6.28	3.12	3.16
December 2	7.91	5.79	2.12

DATA SOURCE: Bloomberg L.P.

Exhibit 4-6 Contrasting the 5- and
10-Year Yields

	10-year	5-year	Slope
February 2	5.71	5.08	0.63
December 2	7.80	7.70	0.10

DATA SOURCE: Bloomberg L.P.

You might have had reason in 1994 to focus on a different seg-ment of the yield curve. Say your area of concern had been the 5-to 10-year maturities (Exhibit 4-6). You can see that that part of the yield curve flattened from 63 basis points to only 10 basis points, a 53-basis-point difference.

Actually, if you look at the November 2 and December 2 yield curves from that year, shown in Exhibit 4-7, you can see that while the four shortest yields continued to rise sharply in response to recent Fed moves, the 5-year yield rose only 7 basis points, and the 10- and 30-year yields both fell. This sample of Treasury yield curves from 1994 illustrates both direct and indirect responses to Fed action.

Supply-Demand
Pressure Counts, Too

Without denying the primacy of Fed policy and inflation concerns as drivers of yield-curve shape, analysts often note that different sectors of the curve seem to have lives of their own. Along with inflation pressure, then, students of the yield curve do well to think about what kinds of investors focus on what parts of the curve. Burton Malkiel has referred to this as "preferred habitats."

Basically, institutional investors choose assets to match liabilities. If one pension fund serves a relatively young workforce, you might expect to see it making longer-term investments. If another serves a relatively aged workforce, you might expect to see it making

Exhibit 4-7 Treasury Yield Curves, November 2, 1994 and December 2, 1994

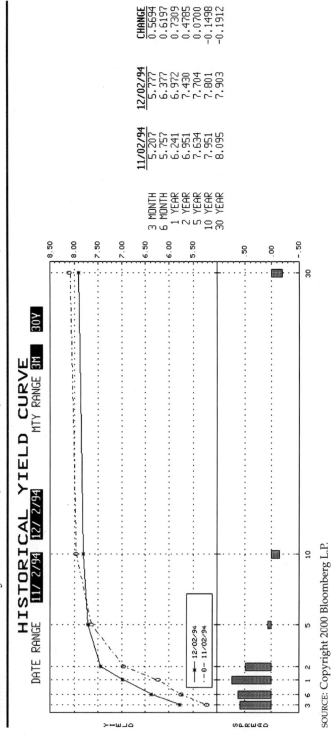

SOURCE: Copyright 2000 Bloomberg L.P.

	11/02/94	12/02/94	CHANGE
3 MONTH	5.207	5.777	0.5694
6 MONTH	5.757	6.377	0.6197
1 YEAR	6.241	6.972	0.7309
2 YEAR	6.951	7.430	0.4785
5 YEAR	7.634	7.704	0.0700
10 YEAR	7.951	7.801	-0.1498
30 YEAR	8.095	7.903	-0.1912

HISTORICAL YIELD CURVE

DATE RANGE 11/ 2/94 12/ 2/94 MTY RANGE 3M 30Y

shorter-term investments. Also, hedging activity tends to concentrate around benchmarks such as bond indexes.

The 5-year sector of the yield curve attracts the securities dealer community, pensions, guaranteed-income contracts (GICs), and, to a lesser extent, banks. GICs, for example, seldom go longer than 5 years. And pension funds measure the success of their managers in terms of benchmarks, most of which have durations that come closest to matching the durations of the 5-year curve sector.

The 10-year sector is dominated by the mortgage security market to such an extent that "no one else counts," in the words of one fund manager. Interestingly, when this sector gets crowded, the mortgage group goes shorter rather than longer and increases pressure on the 5-year sector.

Don't Forget This Is the Information Age

Another factor that plays a bigger role than it did a few years ago is information. Financial news has become big business, and the newspeople can hardly afford to admit that nothing is going on in the markets. This would not sell ad time. More important, electronic technology allows a rapidly growing pool of global capital to link the bond markets of the world.

While it may take 13 hours to fly from Chicago to Japan, money can travel there at the speed of light. This means that the "hot" money of the big hedge funds and other such investors can be transferred from place to place, ever seeking a few extra basis points of yield. The currency market gives a clue to the scope of this market. Daily transaction volume in world currencies amounts to something on the order of $2 trillion. Some of this is trade motivated, of course, but shrewd observers estimate that most of it represents capital flows. The hedge fund managers and others are buying currencies so that they can buy financial instruments—primarily stocks and bonds.

If these are the primary participants in the various yield-curve sectors, then you can get a good start toward understanding yield-curve dynamics by focusing on what drives these businesses. Each is complex and difficult in its own right. Yet attention to such details provides, if not a place to stand and apply a lever, at least a place to start looking.

Credit Supply–Credit Demand

Starting late in 1999, though, investors needed to interpret the U.S. Treasury yield curve with caution, for the curve may have become economic salt that had lost its savor. An inversion in the U.S. Treasury yield curve has presaged a recession or a sharp deceleration in real economic growth throughout most of the postwar period. Because of this, the change in curve shape in early 2000 struck many observers as alarming news. Yet this curve shift may not have carried the usual message.

The message of the yield curve derives from an interesting interplay among economic forces. The shifting relationships between the demand for credit and the creation of credit that the yield curve depicts may provide a useful gauge of the potential for economic growth.

Basically, the long end of the curve, anchored by the benchmark 10-year Treasury note, responds to the demand for credit in the economy. When the demand for credit rises, yields on longer-maturity securities should also rise. When more people want something, the cost tends to rise. Conversely, a diminished demand for credit should lower yields. After all, when fewer people want something, sellers cannot exact a premium for it.

Further, an increasing demand for credit typically goes hand in hand with rising gross domestic product (GDP) growth. People borrow, in the ordinary case, to buy more goods and services. Granted, in recent years, a major cause of borrowing has been the desire of corporations to buy back their own equities rather than the desire to buy goods and services. The general rule still holds.

At the short end of the yield curve, the Fed targets the fed funds rate as a means of regulating the flow of credit into the economy. Within the context of the U.S. economy, the Fed uniquely has the power to create credit.

Accordingly, when the long end of the yield curve is rising relative to the fed funds rate—that is, when the yield curve is steepening—this suggests that an increasing demand for credit is being accommodated by the supply of credit created by the Fed. Conversely, when the long end of the yield curve is falling relative to the fed funds rate—that is, when the yield curve is flattening—this suggests that the Fed is cutting back on the amount of credit it is creating relative to the demand for credit. Thus a steepening yield curve typically has portended faster real economic growth—a flattening yield curve, slower real economic growth.

Looking at the situation the market faced in early 2000, though, you can see an interesting contrast between the behaviors of the 10-year Treasury–fed funds yield spread and the long-term AAA corporate bond–fed funds yield spread. (It is often convenient to look at the difference between two yields—that is, the spread between them—rather than at an entire yield curve. For one thing, this makes plotting history much easier.) During most of the postwar period, as Exhibit 4-8 shows, these two yield spreads shadowed each other closely.

Recently, this has not been the case. Consider that during the period when the Treasury yield curve flattened and eventually inverted and the relevant spread narrowed enormously, the corporate spread narrowed too, but by a more modest amount. Exhibit 4-9 highlights the difference.

The spread using the AAA corporate bond yield has dropped from 238 basis points in late January to 163 basis points in the last week of March—a net narrowing of only 75 basis points in contrast with the 114 basis points of the Treasury–fed funds spread. Not only had this spread narrowed less, it was not even close to going negative. The AAA corporate yield curve, that is, was not even close to inverting.

It is important to try to account for the differing behavior between the two spreads. By implication, the spread between the AAA corporate bond yield and Treasury-note yield has widened since late January. The first thing to consider in trying to explain this is whether there were heightened concerns in early 2000 that AAA-rated corporate bonds would soon be downgraded because of credit issues. However, the spread between top-rated corporate bonds and comparable maturity Treasuries will typically narrow, not widen, just prior to the onset of a recession. Further, there was no evidence at that time that credit concerns were higher than they had been prior to past recessions. This suggests that there must be a reason for the widening of the corporate-to-Treasury yield spread other than credit concerns.

A better explanation for this widening in 2000 was the news about the Treasury's planned buyback that year of $30 billion of its

Exhibit 4-8 Interest Rate Spread (10-Year Bond less Fed Funds Rate) versus Yield Spread (Moody's Aaa Corp. less Fed Funds)

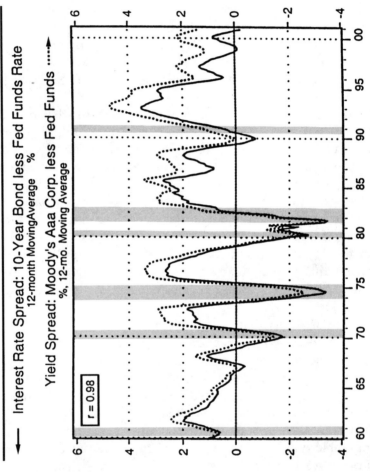

— Interest Rate Spread: 10-Year Bond less Fed Funds Rate
12-month MovingAverage %

····· Yield Spread: Moody's Aaa Corp. less Fed Funds
%, 12-mo. Moving Average

r = 0.98

SOURCE: Bureau of Economic Analysis/Haver Analytics

Exhibit 4-9 Contrasting Yield Spread Narrowing

	Treasury–fed funds (in basis points)	AAA corporate–fed funds (in basis points)
Late January	127	238
Late March	13	163
Difference	114	75

debt of maturities 20 years or more and the cutback in new issues of shorter-maturity debt. These two Treasury policy shifts portended a supply shortage in the market for Treasury securities. This seems to have been the principal factor accounting for the widening in the spread between corporate bonds and Treasury securities and, there-fore, the more extreme narrowing of the Treasury–fed funds spread compared with the AAA corporate–fed funds spread.

Under these circumstances, it would seem preferable to look at the AAA corporate–fed funds spread for information about the future behavior of the economy and whether Fed policy has taken effect. In early 2000, the narrowing of the AAA corporate–fed funds spread foreshadowed some slowing in real economic growth. Yet, with the spread at a relatively lofty 160 basis points, it was hardly issuing the recession alarm that the Treasury yield curve seemed to be sounding.

The Problem with the Treasury Yield Curve As Benchmark

The U.S. Treasury has talked for some time about reducing issuance of longer-dated securities and, just before its February 2000 auction, caused considerable angst in the marketplace by announcing a change in the auction schedule and a buyback program. Because of a series of public relations blunders by high-ranking Treasury offi-cials, the marketplace remains uncertain what the Treasury intends.

A commonplace in the financial markets is that uncertainty breeds volatility. This was certainly shown to be true in the Treasury markets in early 2000. Institutional investors scrambled to buy long-dated issues—seemingly at any price. This supply pressure

considerably warped the yield curve and made it difficult to separate actual interest-rate economics from market frenzy.

The importance of this to anyone trying to plan investment strategy should be obvious. Recent credit spread widening may reflect
not actual changes in credit quality but only this Treasury securities
market volatility.

Further, Treasuries have recently played smaller roles in a number
of portfolios. By early 2000, large and small portfolios representing
banks, pension funds, mutual funds, and foundations tended to
have relatively smaller fractions of their holdings in Treasury securities and relatively large fractions in securities such as high-grade
corporate bonds and mortgage-backed securities, although agency
securities seemed to be a growing part of the whole. Reportedly,
Treasuries were also becoming a smaller fraction of the portfolios
underlying some of the popular benchmark indexes, such as the
Lehman Brothers Aggregate Bond Index. All this makes the idea of
using something other than the Treasury yield curve as a benchmark
for fixed-income investing and as an indicator of future economic
growth sound more and more attractive.

Candidates for benchmark status have included an agency yield
curve—that is, a curve based on the debt issues of such government-sponsored enterprises as Fannie Mae and Freddie Mac—an
AAA corporate yield curve, and a curve based on the fixed rates
used for interest-rate swaps. From the standpoint of ease of use, the
AAA corporate yield curve is the obvious choice.

5

TEDs, TAGs, and the Credit Story

The fed funds rate provides the foundation for any structure for evaluating the state of the U.S. economy. Because the Federal Reserve (Fed) is the supplier of residual credit to the U.S. economy and uses this interest rate to mark the level at which it is willing to supply unlimited credit in cases of excess demand, changes in the fed funds target help define the supply of credit. A yield curve adds a helpful framework in that the relationship between fed funds and 10-year agency debt or AAA corporate bonds gauges the balance between credit supply and demand.

A thriving economy has a healthy appetite for credit, of course. During much of the decade of the 1990s, this seemed to be all that one needed to know—how much the Fed would supply and how much the market wanted. The U.S. stock market seemed to know no direction but up, with the Dow Jones Industrial Average climbing from close to 2,700 in January 1990 to 7,900 in January 1998. To be sure, there were temporary setbacks, like the 1,017-point drop in the Dow during October 1997 (October 7 peak to October 27 trough: 8,178–7,161).

Yet, even when 554 points of it came in a nasty pre-Halloween trick on October 27, 1997, the market didn't worry about the end of the economic expansion. This, after all, was a result of the Asian financial crisis. Those in the know realized that the Fed would take steps to salvage the situation. Inflation was low, which gave the Fed room to maneuver. Professional investors and amateurs alike saw this as a wonderful buying opportunity. They could hardly wait to get back into the market. In a market like this, concerns about the creditworthiness of the borrowers, be they corporations or individuals, stayed deeply buried in the investment community's collective psyche.

Then, in August of 1998, credit concerns surfaced with a vengeance. The Russian credit default combined with the Long-Term Capital Management debacle to spoil the party and bring credit concerns back to the forefront. The stock market remembered that down was a possible direction, and the 20 percent plus gains of the early and middle 1990s evaporated. By the summer of 2000, large numbers of stock mutual funds were reporting year-to-date returns in the 5 percent range.

During the past two decades, the market's concern with credit quality has ebbed and flowed. Not surprisingly, people have devised a variety of market-based tools for evaluating the credit situation, but these, too, have had an up and down record. Yet the market does have things to say about the quality of the credit as well as the overall supply of and appetite for it.

Pricing Credit in the Bond Market

The bond market has always responded to credit concerns. When corporations issue bonds, the market sets the coupons in terms of spreads to comparable maturity Treasuries—the better the credit, the narrower the spread.

To review briefly, remember that bond investors identify bonds in terms of coupon and maturity and price them in terms of yield to maturity. The coupon specifies the annual rate of the semiannual payments the bond issuer makes to the bondholder. For example, the U.S. Treasury issue that figures in the following examples is the 6⅛ percent of August 07. The U.S. Treasury pays holders of such a 10-year note (10 years because it was issued in August 97) 3¹⁄₁₆ percent of its face value every February 15 and August 15 until it matures on August 15, 2007. These interest payments never vary, hence the term *fixed income.*

The yield and price of the bond can and will vary. This constant variation serves investors in an obvious way. Two examples illustrate. Two large U.S. corporations, Ameritech and American Standard, issued 10-year bonds a month apart in 1998. The 6⅛ percent of August 07 was the Treasury benchmark for both issues. The Standard and Poor's (S&P) Ratings Group considered Ameritech to have an AA– credit rating and American Standard to have a BB+. As a result, the Ameritech bond went off at a spread of 72 basis points over the yield of U.S. Treasury securities, which was 5.43 percent at the time, and so has a 6.15 percent coupon. A month later, the American Standard bond went off at a spread of 205 basis points over the Treasury yield, which was 5.575 percent by then. Accordingly, the American Standard bond has a 7⅝ percent coupon. These 72- and 205-basis-point spreads over the Treasury yield amount to the premiums the market demands for taking the credit risk.

Ameritech's AA– rating means that while default is possible, it is highly unlikely. American Standard's BB+ rating, in contrast, means default is an event with a much higher probability. The ratings agencies refer to anything above an S&P BBB– rating as "investment grade" and politely call anything below BBB– "speculative grade." A more common term for bonds rated BB+ and below is *junk bonds.* This credit spread represents the price tag the market is putting on the actuarial risk that the issuer of the bond will fail to make a payment.

Keep in mind that bond prices vary inversely with yields, and this is the mechanism that makes these spreads work. An investor who is nervous about a bond will demand more yield for taking the risk. In effect, this investor is like a department store customer asking for a discount on a garment with a stain or on a piece of furniture with a scratch.

The Plot Thickens

As market conditions change, these credit spreads will change as well. The bonds may still carry their original ratings, but a widening or narrowing spread will tell a more up-to-the-minute story about what the market thinks of that credit. Exhibits 5-1 and 5-2 provide the credit spread record of the Ameritech and American Standard bonds for the 6 months beginning in mid-April 2000.

The upper panel of each exhibit plots the U.S. Treasury yield as a solid line and the corporate yield as a dashed line. You can see at

Exhibit 5-1 Ameritech Bond Yield Spread for April 24, 2000 to October 23, 2000

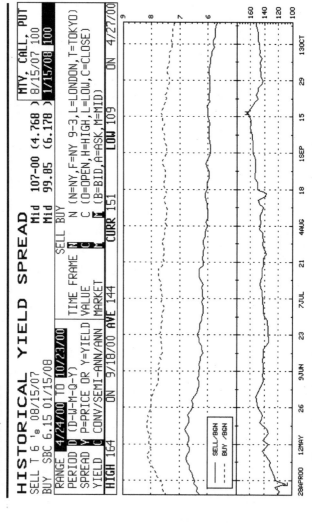

SOURCE: Copyright 2000 Bloomberg L.P.

Exhibit 5-2 American Standard Bond Yield Spread for April 24, 2000 to October 23, 2000

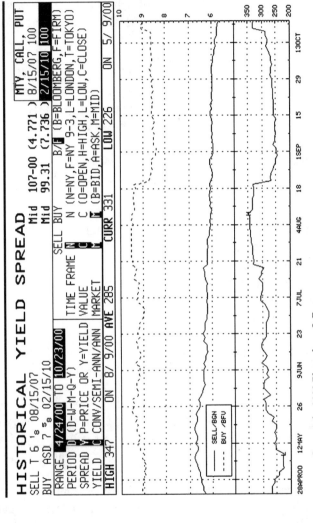

SOURCE: Copyright 2000 Bloomberg L.P.

a glance that the Ameritech spread is far narrower than the American Standard spread. You can also see that by the first date in these snapshots, the spreads were wider than they were at issuance.

The lower panel of each exhibit plots the spread itself, the difference between the corporate and Treasury yields. You can see that the Ameritech spread began these 6 months at 120 basis points, dipped to a low of 109 in April, peaked at 164 in mid-September, and worked back to 151 at the end of this period. This overall upward trend suggests that even though the Ameritech bond retains its AA– rating, the market is growing less happy with this credit—or perhaps with the credit situation in general.

The American Standard spread tells a richer story. Again, the trend is up, and the final 331-basis-point spread is 126 basis points above the spread at issue. But notice the two mesas—a broad one from mid-July to mid-August and one that may be just beginning in mid-October. These suggest that some event, such as a takeover rumor or an earnings disappointment, has made investors nervous. It would take further investigation to determine whether the situation is a temporary concern or a problem of longer duration. Bond investors, though, shoot first and investigate later, which is what makes these spreads helpful.

Useful as these spreads can be to professional investors, they have shortcomings for individuals. Corporate bonds can be terribly illiquid. In looking for candidates for these two examples, a number of attractive ones turned up on the quote screen with the terse notation, "Not priced." This means that there hasn't been a trade in these bonds for some time. The last yield, whenever it was, may no longer be relevant. Quite apart from that, this information is not easily accessible to the average individual investor.

You might well wonder why the fuss. What, after all, are the credit ratings agencies for? Granted, the credit ratings agencies such as Moody's and Standard & Poor's issue credit ratings based on their evaluations of individual companies. Yet the investment community has not always been completely happy with such estimates.

For example, several large companies suffered major angst because of troubled derivatives transactions during 1994. At the time, professional investors criticized the ratings agencies for being slow to spot the problems. Whether the criticisms were fair and justified remains an open question.

What is clear is that the markets want more up-to-date information than what the ratings agencies can supply. You can see from the Ameritech and American Standard examples that during a period when the ratings of these two issues remained stable, the market's sense of the two credits changed a great deal. While there are several ways to figure out the market consensus on these issues, the futures market generates useful and easily accessible information in this regard.

The Original TED Spread

The first futures market attempt to capture this credit dynamic emerged in the early 1980s when Eurodollar futures began trading at the Chicago Mercantile Exchange (Merc). Eurodollar futures, known among futures traders as *EDs*, derive from 3-month Eurodollar time deposits. These are U.S. dollar–denominated deposits held in foreign banks. Because these time deposits are issued by unregulated banks—or at least banks not subject to U.S. regulation—their yields are thought to reflect a risk premium over 3-month Treasury-bill rates, which anchor the short end of the U.S. Treasury yield curve. Thus, in terms of credit risk, or the risk of credit issuer default, the Treasury-ED (TED) spread plays risky debt off against nonrisky Treasury debt.

The futures market works in terms of price; the rest of the financial world, in terms of yield. Fortunately, the conversion is easy for instruments such as Treasury bills (T-bills) and EDs. To go from yield to price, for either instrument, subtract the yield from 100.

T-bill yield	T-bill price
100 − 6.16	= 93.84

To go from price to yield, subtract the price from 100.

ED price	ED yield
100 − 92.38	= 7.62

The TED spread, simply enough, amounts to the T-bill price minus the ED price, assuming the same contract month. Thus, with June 2000 T-bill futures quoted at 93.84 and the June 2000 ED trading at 92.38 on May 18, 2000, the TED was 1.46, or 146 basis points.

T-bill price	ED price	TED spread
93.84 − 92.38 =		1.46

You can just as easily calculate the TED in yield terms if you remember to reverse the order of subtraction.

ED yield	T-bill yield	TED spread
7.62 − 6.16 =		1.46

The spread on May 18, 2000 was the same 146 basis points either way.

The early days of the TED provide good examples both of how such an indicator might function and of what can happen to render the signal essentially useless. The TED provided a means for investors to express views about how risky EDs were as opposed to T-bills. The situation in the early 1980s, with regard to the dynamics of the U.S. capital markets, focused a great deal of attention on the money center banks and the political and economic events that could put them at risk. These banks were the primary sources of credit for businesses large and small, and their soundness was a crucial factor in evaluating the state of the U.S. economy.

With no danger looming on the economic or political horizons, investors will naturally welcome the risk of EDs and other risky debt to gain the extra yield. Heavier buying of EDs, relative to the buying of T-bills, will force up the price of Eurodollars and push down their yield—in relative terms—to narrow the TED.

Conversely, the threat of political unrest or economic trouble might well make investors shy away from Eurodollars. Suppose that they actually pull money out of Eurodollar and other risky deposits and transfer it to T-bills. This "flight to quality" will drive Eurodollar prices down at the same time it pushes T-bill prices higher. This will widen the TED.

This is exactly what happened in May of 1984 when Chicago's Continental Illinois Bank was teetering on the brink of failure. At the time, most of the money center banks were trying to cope with mountains of bad loans, and indeed, the entire U.S. banking system appeared to be on shaky ground. Investors, nervous about their exposure to this situation because of having money in uninsured time deposits, fled Eurodollars and embraced T-bills. Their action drove the TED far wider, as Exhibit 5-3 shows, to a peak of slightly over 200 basis points—more than 100 basis points over what it had been at the first of that year.

It is important to notice that the TED climbed all spring—issuing a warning to all who knew enough to heed it.

What happened next eventually killed the traditional 3-month TED as a useful market indicator. The U.S. government let it be known that it considered Continental Bank and the other money center banks "too big to fail." The basic idea was that these money center banks were too crucial to the entire U.S. financial system to be allowed to go down. It didn't matter if these banks were making loans of questionable quality or performing something less than due diligence in their credit checks. These banks, the government thought, could not be allowed to go down.

This government policy stance took the danger out of uninsured deposits. Investors reasoned that the extra yield was worth it, no matter what was going on politically and economically. Even if the bank did make foolish loans to oil wildcatters or to unstable Latin American governments, it wouldn't matter. The government would step in to bail out the bank and make the investors whole.

Along with this policy blow to the TED, the T-bill futures market fell victim to the success of Eurodollar futures, and liquidity dried up until the T-bill futures market all but died. By the early 1990s, a standard joke around the futures markets was that bad as T-bill liquidity had gotten, the only way anyone could trade as much as 100 contracts of T-bill futures (a paltry amount for institutional investors who routinely trade in thousands of contracts) would be to trade a TED spread and offset the ED side. A researcher for one house at the time flatly declared, "The TED is dead."

Exhibit 5-3 TED Spread, 1982–1988

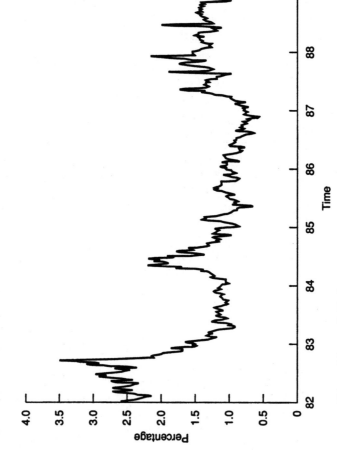

SOURCE: Chicago Mercantile Exchange

Eventually, the situation reached the point where the traditional 3-month futures TED dried up and blew away, for all practical purposes. Should you use cash market data to replicate the TED, what you would see is that sometime around 1989 or 1990, the TED got "very quiet," in the words of another market research specialist, and stayed that way.

The Market Took a Longer Look at the TED

This does not mean that the market cannot provide interesting insights into what it thinks of the credit quality of U.S. debt issuers. Investors and market analysts still watch and trade the TED in the over-the-counter market. What they use, though, is not the traditional 3-month TED but rather 2- and 5-year *term TEDs*. These longer-dated TEDs are based on ideas borrowed from the market for interest-rate swaps, which has become a mainstay of corporate finance.

An *interest-rate swap* is simply an agreement between two parties to exchange interest-rate payments every 3 or 6 months. Unlike a bond or other loan, where both principal and interest payments change hands, the principal amount named in a swap deal is a *notional* principal—a reference number to use for determining the size of the interest payments. One of the payments is based on a floating interest rate—usually the 3- or 6-month London InterBank Offered Rate (LIBOR), an interest rate that has become the standard reference point for most business lending. The other interest rate is a fixed one, usually the relevant-maturity U.S. Treasury benchmark plus a spread. For a 5-year swap, this would be the most recently issued 5-year Treasury note, as it would for a corporate bond issue.

What made term TEDs possible was the swap market's discovery, early on, that it could use sequences of ED futures, called *strips*, to replicate a swap. This created a risk-management tool well suited to the needs of the swap dealers and other market users and resulted in EDs developing incredible liquidity out to 5 years or a bit more.

The term TEDs are based on the same idea. It is possible to create a synthetic Eurobond using a strip of ED futures. The term TED, then, will be the difference between the Treasury price and the price of the synthetic Eurobond. Exhibits 5-4 and 5-5 show plots of the 2- and 5-year term TEDs from June 1994 to June 2000.

You can see that the markets showed little concern about credit quality until the summer of 1998. Ever since then, the markets have been extremely sensitive to credit quality issues. As a result, the spread has been volatile from that time forward.

Term TEDs Reflect Market Concerns

A strength of these term TEDs is that they focus attention on maturities of major concern to bond market investors. Corporations issue a great deal of this medium-term debt, and pension and insurance company portfolios hold huge amounts of bonds at these maturities.

Life insurance company portfolio managers must perform an interesting balancing act. The regulations within which they must operate restrict them to investment-grade assets, yet they want to generate as much yield as possible to fund their liabilities. As a result, in the words of a risk-management specialist for one such firm, these portfolio managers "live in 5-year BBB– country," that being the highest-yielding paper that still qualifies as investment grade. Balancing on the edge of permissibility like this, such portfolio managers have to be especially careful with regard to the credit question. The TEDs, then, reflect the concerns or, better, the anticipated concerns of these investors.

The operation of term TEDs is the same as that of the traditional 3-month TED. When all is well politically and economically, investors prefer riskier debt because of its higher yield. When trouble threatens, they tend to put new money in safer places such as U.S. Treasury securities. This flight to quality will widen the spread. Better times will motivate capital flows back into riskier investments and narrow the spread.

The TEDs respond to these capital flows for three reasons. Investors concerned about what these developments will do to their holdings may use the term TEDs to shift from a riskier, longer-dated position to a relatively safer, shorter-dated position and so tem-

Exhibit 5-4 Two-Year TED Spread

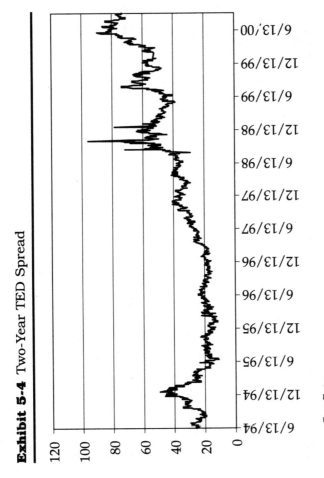

SOURCE: Carr Futures

Exhibit 5-5 Five-Year TED Spread

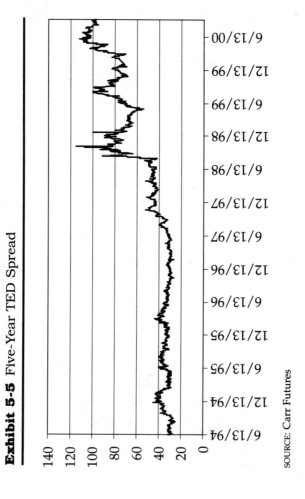

SOURCE: Carr Futures

porarily alter the risk profiles of their portfolios. A second set of concerned investors may use term TEDs to hedge their credit-spread exposure, which is another kind of risk profile adjustment. A third set may simply take positions on the credit-spread situation. That is, they may believe that economic or political events will unfold in the next few months such that the spread will narrow significantly. They may believe the market has overdone its credit concerns. For example, the October 23, 2000 *BondWeek* quoted a portfolio manager as saying, "The bond market has overdone concerns about credit quality, which has sent spreads on many bonds to the widest levels since the crises of 1998." Whatever the specifics and completely apart from their other holdings, they may decide to take positions on these outlooks.

When these investors see any factor on the horizon that might threaten the ability of debt issuers to meet their obligations, the term TEDs will reflect those concerns. You can see in Exhibits 5-4 and 5-5 that the volatility did not happen all at once when the Long-Term Capital Management troubles surfaced. These TEDs began signaling trouble well in advance of that.

A weakness of these TEDs is that they are hard to track for anyone lacking the analytical tools of the professionals. Brokerages often maintain such data as the exhibits show, but this is not the same as finding quotes in a newspaper or on a screen and doing a simple calculation.

TAG Spreads Tell the Same Story As Term TEDs

The information about the market's perceptions of the credit situation embodied in term TEDs now has a futures market counterpart. The spread between 5- and 10-year agency note futures and U.S. Treasury note futures at those maturities, known as *Treasury-agency (TAG) spreads*, tells essentially the same credit spread story as term TEDs.

The agency futures derive from a deliverable set of Fannie Mae Benchmark Notes[SM] and Freddie Mac Reference Notes[SM]. These two government-sponsored enterprises (GSEs) issue, or reopen, these notes according to a regular auction schedule, much like Treasury issuance, and use them to finance their mortgage lending activities. It is important to realize that these are not mortgage securities but noncallable, coupon-paying issues—much like the Treasury securities deliverable into the Treasury futures contracts.

However, as the Treasury has tried to make clear on several recent occasions, the GSEs are not government agencies (like Ginnie Mae) and so do not have the "full faith and credit" backing of the U.S. government. In street parlance, they are agencies anyway. Acknowledging the fact that their debt is defaultable, though, the market prices these issues at a spread to U.S. Treasury securities, just as it does corporate bonds. Essentially, to the market, these are AAA credits.

Calculating the TAG Spread

The TAG spread is slightly less easy to calculate than the original TED but far easier to calculate than term TEDs. The slight difficulty comes from the fact that agency and Treasury securities are quoted in points and thirty-seconds of 100 percent. A price of 101-20 means one hundred one and twenty thirty-seconds percent of par. (When the coupon and yield of a fixed-income security match, the price is 100-00, or par. These securities always pay par at maturity.) At this 101-20 price, a $10 million par position would have a dollar value of $10,162,500.

Figuring out such a dollar equivalent, or calculating a TAG spread, requires conversions of thirty-seconds into decimal equivalents and, perhaps, conversions of decimals back into thirty-seconds. In this example, $20/32$ is equivalent to 0.625 (20/32 = 0.625). To go the other way, simply multiply a decimal fraction by 32 (0.625 × 32 = 20).

Suppose that 10-year Treasury futures are trading at 101-20, while 10-year agency futures are trading at 95-31. This makes the 10-year TAG 5-21. Exhibit 5-6 takes you through the steps.

The TAG spread, like any credit spread, can move independently of yield levels, and such spreads are sometimes more volatile than interest rates.

Exhibit 5-6 Calculating a 10-Year TAG Spread

	Quoted price	Convert 32nds to decimals	Subtract decimal prices
Treasury	101-20	20/32 = 0.625	101.625
Agency	95-31	31/32 = 0.96875	−95.96875
			5.65625
		Convert decimals to 32nds	
TAG	5-21	0.65625 × 32 = 21	

DATA SOURCE: Chicago Board of Trade

In general, the credit component and the interest-rate component in a corporate yield are separate. The interest-rate component responds to credit supply and demand and inflation concerns, just as Treasury yields do. The credit component responds to concerns about the overall business climate and any other factors that may affect the issuer's ability to service its debt. While this is not completely separate from the interest-rate situation, the credit spread can seem quite independent of interest rates.

Typically, when interest rates are falling, the market considers such issuers to be more easily able to fulfill their debt obligations, that is, to be less likely to default. Then the credit spreads should narrow, although they may do so at a different rate than the rate of fall in interest rates.

At times, though, interest rates and credit spreads can move in opposite directions. In the fall of 1998, for example, U.S. Treasury rates were falling sharply, but credit spreads were widening. Concerns about fallout from the Russian credit default and the Long-Term Capital Management situation created widespread concerns about credit quality. Indeed, credit spreads have remained relatively volatile ever since.

Relating TAGs and TEDs

You can see from Exhibit 5-7 that the 10-year TAG spread tracks the 10-year swap spread closely. In addition, Exhibit 5-8 shows that the

Exhibit 5-7 10-Year TAG Spread versus 10-Year Swap Spread

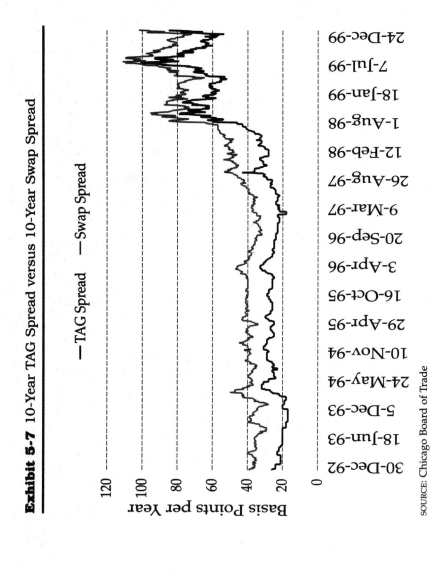

— TAG Spread   — Swap Spread

Basis Points per Year

120 — 100 — 80 — 60 — 40 — 20 — 0

30-Dec-92 · 18-Jun-93 · 5-Dec-93 · 24-May-94 · 10-Nov-94 · 29-Apr-95 · 16-Oct-95 · 3-Apr-96 · 20-Sep-96 · 9-Mar-97 · 26-Aug-97 · 12-Feb-98 · 1-Aug-98 · 18-Jan-99 · 7-Jul-99 · 24-Dec-99

SOURCE: Chicago Board of Trade

Exhibit 5-8 5-Year TAG Spread

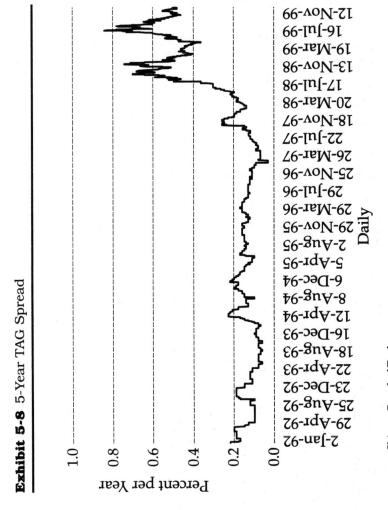

Percent per Year

Daily

1.0

0.8

0.6

0.4

0.2

0.0

2-Jan-92
29-Apr-92
25-Aug-92
23-Dec-92
22-Apr-93
18-Aug-93
16-Dec-93
12-Apr-94
8-Aug-94
6-Dec-94
5-Apr-95
2-Aug-95
29-Nov-95
29-Mar-96
29-Jul-96
25-Nov-96
26-Mar-97
22-Jul-97
18-Nov-97
20-Mar-98
17-Jul-98
13-Nov-98
19-Mar-99
16-Jul-99
12-Nov-99

SOURCE: Chicago Board of Trade

77

5-year TAG spread strongly resembles the 5-year TED spread (shown in Exhibit 5-5).

The advantage of term TEDs is that they have an obvious connection to the swap market because of their LIBOR-based Eurodollar components. Yet Exhibits 5-7 and 5-8 show that TAGs provide essentially the same information as term TEDs. This, plus their greater accessibility, seems to make them an ideal tool for evaluation of the credit situation.

6

Volatility— An Indicator of Market Potential

Market outlooks tend to concentrate on market direction—whether the current trend will continue and when the direction might change. Important as this can be, you may also want to know how far the trend will continue or, if the market breaks, how far could it reasonably go against your position. You want at least to know what the probabilities for such moves might be.

An analyst may say that the present stock market rally has only a little topside potential left. If your strategy calls for selling a portion of your holdings when the market strikes you as having gone as high as it will go for now—in market jargon, when it has *neared a top*—you might plausibly ask how much is "only a little."

Similarly, if you are about to enter into a short-term trade—buying a stock or an index to take advantage of an economic event of some kind—you might wonder how much the market is likely to move in a given period. In seeking answers to questions such as these, you can benefit from a study of volatility.

Volatility has an everyday language sense and a more technical market use. When market commentators refer to a volatile stock market, for example, they most often mean simply that the market has been behaving like the one shown in Exhibit 6-1.

You can look at a chart like this one and see that this market has indeed been bouncing around, and the bounces have been large enough to take your breath away. But to say that this market is

Exhibit 6-1 Dow Jones Industrial Average, March 15, 2000 to September 14, 2000

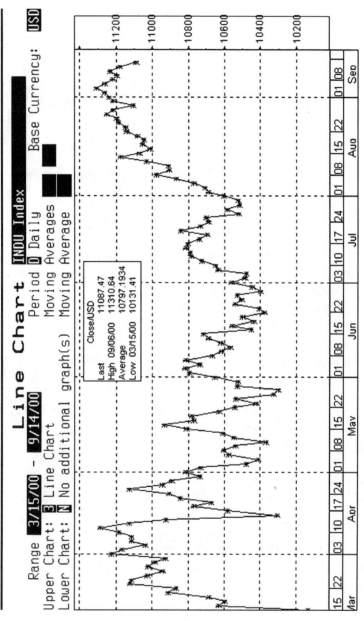

SOURCE: Copyright 2000 Bloomberg L.P.

volatile in this sense is a gee-whiz fact. You can note it, but you can't put it to work for you.

Volatility has a more technical side that can be both observed and put to work. Most of the insights that make volatility useful come from the options markets. While discussions of options can get extremely technical, you can easily develop a rough and ready sense of volatility that can be of great help to you in thinking about your investment tactics.

Simply put, volatility measures the opportunity inherent in the present market. Of course, the flip side of opportunity is risk. Of primary interest here is the fact that from a study of volatility, you can develop a useful sense of how far the market professionals think their market can move in a given time interval.

Looking Back and Looking Forward

Market professionals look at two kinds of volatility—historical and implied. Unfortunately, the print media do not list volatilities for stocks, indexes, or commodities. Most quotation services do list them, and brokers will often supply them if you ask.

Indeed, many quotation services chart volatilities for you. The charts in Exhibits 6-2a through c show the two kinds of volatility in relation to the relevant futures prices for three rather different futures markets—the ones derived from the Dow Jones Industrial Average (DJIA or Dow), the 10-year Treasury note, and crude oil.

Even a casual glance calls attention to the difference between the two kinds of volatility. Notice how the 10-day historical plot dips and soars while the implied plot follows a steadier path in all three cases.

As the term indicates, *historical volatility* involves looking back at recent market history. Analysts take the daily price differences for, say, the last 10 days and perform a statistical analysis of them. They express the result in annualized percentage terms. With Dow futures trading at 11,047, your quotation service might list a 10-day historical volatility of 12.50 percent.

This means, based on 10 days of history, that there is a two-thirds (68 percent) probability that the Dow futures level 1 year from the day of this reading will lie somewhere along a band plus or minus

Exhibit 6-2a Volatility in the Dow Jones Industrial Average (DJZO)

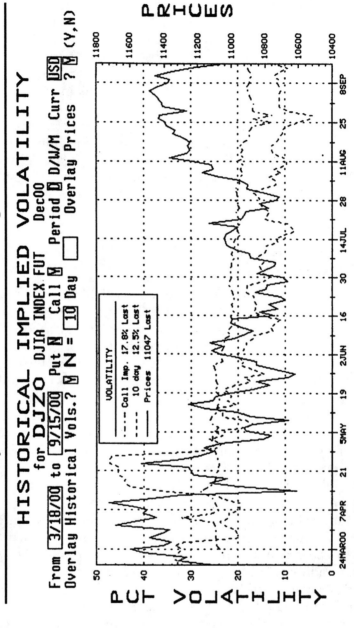

SOURCE: Copyright 2000 Bloomberg L.P.

Exhibit 6-2b Volatility in the 10-Year Treasury Note (TYZO)

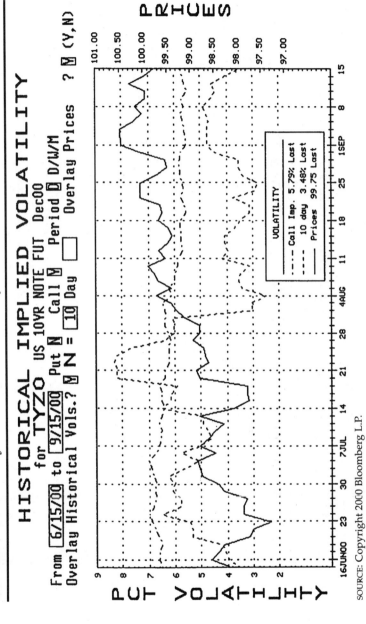

SOURCE: Copyright 2000 Bloomberg L.P.

Exhibit 6-2c Volatility in Crude Oil (CLZ0)

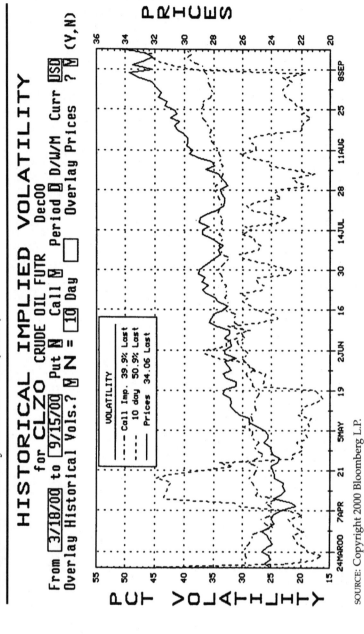

SOURCE: Copyright 2000 Bloomberg L.P.

12.50 percent of the current level. That is, given the data cited, there is a two-thirds probability that the Dow 1 year from now will be trading somewhere between 12,428 and 9,666.

Many quotation services also show a *call implied volatility*. A call option conveys the right, but not the obligation, to buy a stock or a futures contract at a specified price, known as a *strike price*, any time until expiration of the option. Five factors determine the option price, or the premium, you must pay for this right: the underlying market price, the strike price, the financing rate, the number of days to expiration, and the volatility.

Suppose that you want to buy a call on DJIA futures that will give you the right to buy the futures at 11,000 any time in the next 101 days. With the underlying market at 11,047, a financing rate of 6.43 percent, and 11.50 percent 10-day historical volatility, the option pricing model will generate a 30.75 price, or premium. Suppose that you look at a quote screen and see that the market is quoting a 42.75 price for this call. Analysts can use this price to back into a volatility figure. In this case, all other data the same, the 42.75 price "implies" a 17.80 percent volatility. Hence the term *implied volatility*.

The significance of this 5.3 percentage point volatility difference should be obvious. With the market at 11,047, this suggests that 1 year from now there is a two-thirds probability that the Dow will lie somewhere in a range bounded by 13,013 on the upside and 9,081 on the downside. Exhibit 6-3 summarizes the ranges these two volatilities define.

This exhibit shows that the higher implied volatility suggests more upside opportunity but also more downside risk.

Exhibit 6-3 Contrasting Views of Market Potential

	Volatility	
	Historical 12.50%	Implied 17.80%
Upside	12,428	13,013
Market	11,047	11,047
Downside	9,666	9,081
Range	2,762	3,932

DATA SOURCE: Bloomberg L.P.

Importantly, the contrast between these historical and implied volatilities suggests that professional traders see more danger in this market than recent history indicates. The higher quoted price of the option includes a risk premium—a margin of safety for the market makers.

This is helpful information because it gives you a quick read on how much danger the market professionals foresee. In this case, they think the market is more dangerous than it looks. The converse could be true as well. At times, the market could see less danger than history suggests.

Scaling Volatility Information to Your Investment Horizon

Still, such a yearlong horizon may not tell you what you need to know. Suppose that you hold a diversified portfolio of stocks and want to know what could happen to the stock market during the next 60 days. Knowing that the Dow is trading at 11,047 and that the implied volatility is 17.80 percent, you can derive information appropriate to your time horizon by means of a simple arithmetic process.

To determine what the market says about the potential of the market, you must first determine how many 60-day periods there are in a year:

$$365/60 = 6.08$$

Next, find the square root of that number:

$$\sqrt{6.08} = 2.47$$

Divide the implied volatility (expressed in decimal terms) by that square root:

$$0.178/2.47 = 0.0721$$

Multiply the current price (or index level) by that factor:

$$11,047 \times 0.0721 = 796$$

Finally, add and subtract that result to and from the current price:

$$11,047 + 796 = 11,843$$

$$11,047 - 796 = 10,251$$

From this you can see that there is a two-thirds probability the market level 60 days forward will fall somewhere between 11,843 and 10,251.

Notice that volatility makes no claim about market direction. Nor does it make any claim about where in the range the price will fall. It only says that two times in three, the price will land somewhere in that range.

Still, this seems worth knowing. Suppose that on October 15, a highly regarded mutual fund manager tells a TV audience that she expects a 13,000 Dow by year-end. Given the same 11,047 Dow level and 17.80 percent implied volatility and a 77-day period from October 15 to December 31, you can see that 13,000 could be on the optimistic side. This exercise suggests a two-thirds probability that the level will fall between 11,950 and 10,144. The 13,000 prediction could turn out to be accurate, but it is a lower-probability event.

You may recognize the two-thirds probability used here as covering plus or minus 1 standard deviation. You can increase the projection to 2 standard deviations by doubling the amount you add to and subtract from the price at the end of this sequence. This increases the probability to about 95 percent.

In any market situation, you should bear in mind that whatever can happen probably will—at some time. The 1987 stock market crash was an incredibly low probability event, yet it happened.

A More Advanced Idea

Follow an option market for a few weeks and you'll soon realize that option price changes do not match price changes in the underlying commodity or index one for one. Rather, they change in a ratio, and the term option traders use to define this ratio is *delta*.

Keep in mind that the buyer of an American-style call option has the right, but not the obligation, to buy the underlying security for a specified price, called the *strike* or *exercise price*, any time up to option expiration. Similarly, the buyer of a put option has the same kind of right to sell the security. The price the option buyer pays for this right is called the *premium*.

Consider options on 10-year U.S. Treasury futures, for example. With the futures trading at par, or 100-00, 73 days to option expiration, and implied volatility at 5.69 percent, the 100 call has a price of 1-00, the 101 call has a price of 0-38, and the 102 call has a price of 0-21. Suppose that with 60 days to option expiration you decide to buy the 102 call at 0-21.

U.S. Treasury security prices are expressed as a percentage of par, and the fractions are thirty-seconds of a percentage point. That is, a price of 101-16 is $101\frac{16}{32}$ percent of par, par being 100 percent, or 100-00. The way the pricing for Treasury securities, or any fixed-income securities, works is that when the coupon rate equals the yield, the price will be 100-00, which is par. Also, fixed-income securities pay holders par at maturity. Option prices use a similar notation except that the fractions are sixty-fourths. That is, a Treasury option price of 0-38 indicates $\frac{38}{64}$ of a percentage point.

One futures contract promises delivery of $100,000 par of a given U.S. Treasury security. Similarly, an option on that futures contract exercises into one futures contract. Accordingly, a futures contract priced at 101-16 has a cash equivalent value of $101,500, while the option priced at 0-38 will cost $593.80 (38/64 = 0.5938; 0.5938 × 1,000 = 593.80). It follows that the 102 call priced at 0-21 will cost $328.10 (21/64 = 0.3281; 0.3281 × 1,000 = 328.10).

Option traders use a derivative of the option price called *delta* to predict how much the option price will change for a given change in the underlying futures or security price. In options market terminology, an option with a strike price exactly the same as the price of the underlying futures or security is said to be *at the money*. A call option with a strike price higher than the price of the underlying future or security is said to be *out of the money*. A call option with a strike price lower than the price of the underlying futures or security is said to be *in the money*.

The option pricing formula determines the delta of an at-the-money call to be 0.50. This value is determined by the pricing model. A 0.50 delta predicts that the option price will change $\frac{1}{2}$ point for every 1-point change in the price of the underlying futures or security. As call options go farther out of the money, the deltas move toward zero. As options go farther into the money, the deltas move toward one.

Exhibit 6-4 shows how the prices of the 100, 101, and 102 calls on 10-year Treasury futures will react to a 1-point futures price move, from 100-00 to 101-00, after 7 days have passed.

Notice that the deltas in this exhibit approximate the percentage change in the three option prices. The slight differences seen here result from the fact that this price change occurred with 66 days left to option expiration. As a result, several factors beyond the scope of this discussion come into play.

While predicting option price change is the primary function of deltas, deltas also provide rough estimates of the probability that the underlying market will reach a level at least slightly beyond the strike price.

Technically, a 0.38 delta, in this example the delta of the 101 call on 10-year Treasury futures, indicates a 38 percent probability that this call will expire in the money. This is not to say that the 101 call is very likely to be profitable, for a number of other factors come into play. It only says that there is a 38 percent probability that the futures will be trading at least slightly higher than 101-00 when this option expires.

Turning this around, you can use option deltas to gauge, in a rough and ready way, the probability that the market will reach a certain level. You can see how this can be of practical use by going back to the analyst's prediction of a 13,000 Dow by year-end. Given the current 17.80 percent implied volatility, you already know that a 13,000 Dow is a low-probability event, but you can refine this conclusion even more.

Given current market conditions, a 13,000 Dow call, which is far out of the money, has a 0.07 delta. That is, the options market suggests

Exhibit 6-4 Delta Predicts Price Change

Option strike price	Initial price	Delta	Final price	Price change	Percentage change
100	1-00	0.50	1-34	0-34	53
101	0-38	0.38	0-62	0-24	37
102	0-21	0.24	0-36	0-15	23

DATA SOURCE: Bloomberg L.P.

a 7 percent probability that the Dow will at least slightly surpass the 13,000 level by December 31. This certainly underscores the earlier claim that the analyst's prediction is a low-probability event.

A word of caution is in order, though. Any of these volatility- and delta-based estimates of where a market might go result from what the market sees and thinks today. In the days and weeks to come, new factors may emerge that can change volatilities, prices, and deltas. The market evaluates these factors on a continuing basis, and you should do the same as you monitor your investing strategies.

More than this, the quantitative measures of the options world go only so far. A number of years ago, Ezra Zask, a veteran currency trader, said, "You have to remember that in these markets, whatever can happen probably will." For example, options experts have said that the 1987 stock market crash was a 27-standard-deviation event. This is another way of saying that it was a once-in-a-century event. Yet it happened. In 1989, there was another market shock that was almost as severe, and in 1997, the Dow lost 900 points during the month of October. This looks like three once-in-a-century events in one decade.

As volatility increases, such events seem to gain in likelihood. The currency market offers a case in point. In the summer of 1992, the Deutsche mark became extremely volatile. While the two-thirds probability (plus or minus 1 standard deviation) band of the volatility exercise covered the movements in the stock, bond, and energy markets that summer, even the 2-standard-deviation band, which offers a 99 percent probability, failed to contain the gyrations of the German currency. Followers of this market will recall that virtually all European currencies came under extreme stress, and there was a major currency crisis in September 1992.

In sum, the volatility and delta indicators are helpful guides but not hard and fast promises of things to come.

A Note on the Psychology of Volatility

Although an implied volatility of 17.80 percent seems significantly higher than the 12.50 percent 10-day historical volatility, *high* is a relative term. Keep in mind that until roughly the first of June 2000,

Dow implied volatility was trading around 25 percent. In this context, the late-summer 17.80 percent seems relatively low and suggests that the market is currently a somewhat safer place to be.

Because either kind of volatility captures a market response to an economic situation, it seems useful to consider briefly the psychology of the market with regard to volatility.

In the financial markets, falling prices tend to drive up volatility, while in physical markets, such as the grains or oil, rising prices have the same effect. The logic of this is not hard to discover if you ask what kinds of situations are likely to make people nervous in any of these markets. Volatility, after all, measures how agitated the market is at a given time based on the information available, and markets get agitated when people lack knowledge or fear the worst.

For an investor in stocks, the worst is a stock price dropping substantially below the purchase price, dropping low enough to cut off the dividend stream, or even dropping to zero. Logically enough, when the stock market is on the rise, or at least holding steady, none of these worries surface. Then option market makers see little need to charge much in the way of a risk premium, and volatility trends lower.

Conversely, when the market is falling rapidly, people begin to worry about earnings reports, the competence of management to preserve shareholder value, and the health of their own portfolios. Money managers often move in ways that, in hindsight, appear rash and panic-driven. The result is that market makers increase the premiums they charge, and volatility increases.

Similar things happen in the world of fixed-income securities. There, of course, prices vary inversely with interest rates. Falling prices mean rising interest rates, in which case investors begin to wonder whether bond issuers can meet interest payments, how the Fed will respond, and whether their holdings can still beat the benchmark against which their performance is judged. These worries manifest themselves, again, in higher volatility.

In contrast, higher prices in the physical commodities are the danger signals. Perhaps the highest volatility ever seen in the energy markets emerged in the days immediately following the Iraqi invasion of Kuwait in the summer of 1990. Crude oil prices, and the prices of such products as gasoline, jet fuel, and heating oil, shot up, and volatility soared as well. This seems natural enough. Just at a time when a large and largely unanticipated military mobilization in response to the Iraqi invasion created extra demand for crude oil and the products distilled from it, major sources of supply were shut off or severely threatened. The fear of a possible supply shortage can be as bad as an actual loss of supply in a case such as this.

In short, in the case of physical commodities, sharply rising prices typically signal supply crises or the anticipation of them. When the market fears that there will not be enough oil, corn, or copper to go around, it responds in an agitated way, and volatility increases. Conversely, when supplies are plentiful and supply lines are open and flowing smoothly, no one has cause for worry, prices fall, and volatility dips.

Volatility Can Help with Timing

In early September 2000, you might have been thinking about buying one or several airline stocks. Say that you narrowed your choices, for whatever reasons, to three: Airborne Freight (ABF), Delta Airlines (DAL), and United Airlines (UAL). You may have noticed, as Exhibit 6-5 shows, that all three were trading at or near their 52-week lows by mid-month.

One of the questions you face concerns whether this is a good time to buy or whether these stocks might yet have some downside potential. You do not especially want to buy Delta at 48.25, for example, only to see it plunge to 40. At the same time, you do not want to delay buying only to see the price climb right out of your price range. A consideration of the volatility of these stocks and of heating oil futures, oddly enough, can at least help you think about the trade-offs such decisions entail.

Exhibit 6-5 Airline Stock Prices and Volatilities

	Price	52-Week range	Implied volatility
ABF	14	14–26.88	38.33
DAL	48.25	43.56–58.31	36.28
UAL	46.75	45.75–79	26.22

DATA SOURCE: Bloomberg L.P.

Why Heating Oil Is Relevant

Fuel is the big variable cost for transportation companies, so their stocks can be extremely sensitive to oil prices—especially airline stocks. However, the relationship tends to be an inverse one. Sharply rising fuel prices tend to drive down the share prices of these companies. Exhibits 6-6a through d show what was happening to the stock prices of the three airlines during a time of sharply rising heating oil prices.

Granted, airlines use jet kerosene (or jet kero) for fuel, not heating oil. Yet jet kero, diesel fuel, and heating oil are all medium distillates and come, as the oil people say, from the same part of the barrel in the refining process. As a result, heating oil futures can serve as a useful proxy for all three products—at least for an exercise such as this one. The news from market analysts, and even the nonspecialist newspapers, in early September 2000 was that fuel prices were likely to go higher during the next several months.

Knowing this, you might look at heating oil prices and volatility and consider what that information suggests about what might happen to fuel prices in the next 2 months. This, in turn, can shape your thinking about whether now is the time to buy the stocks of these three airline companies. Exhibit 6-7 shows the relationship between heating oil prices and volatilities.

On September 5, 2000, December heating oil futures were trading at 96.35 cents a gallon, and the implied volatility of the at-the-money call was 42.45 percent. This indicates a two-thirds probability that the early November price of heating oil would fall somewhere between $1.1252 per gallon and $0.8018 per gallon. Exhibit 6-8 shows the arithmetic.

According to the options market, the delta of the 112 December call was 0.268. This translates into a 27 percent probability that the market expects the 112 call to expire in the money. Recall that *in the money* means that the futures price at expiration will be at least a few cents higher than 112.

This tells you that, to the extent that they track heating oil prices, jet fuel prices could have quite a bit of upside potential. A 27 percent probability is nowhere close to a sure thing, but it makes $1.12 seem like a real possibility. The question that remains concerns what, if anything, this tells you about the downside potential of these stocks.

Exhibit 6-6a Airborne Freight (ABF) Stock Prices

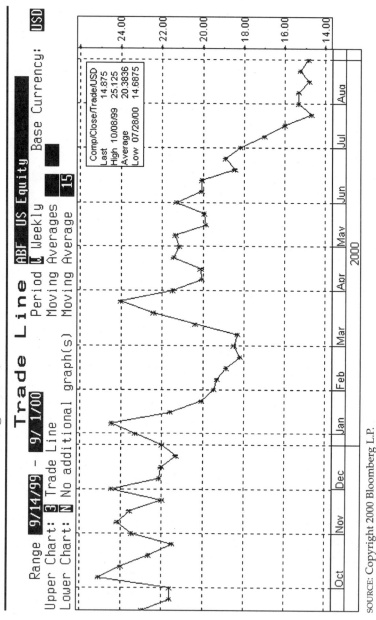

SOURCE: Copyright 2000 Bloomberg L.P.

Exhibit 6-6b Delta Airlines (DAL) Stock Prices

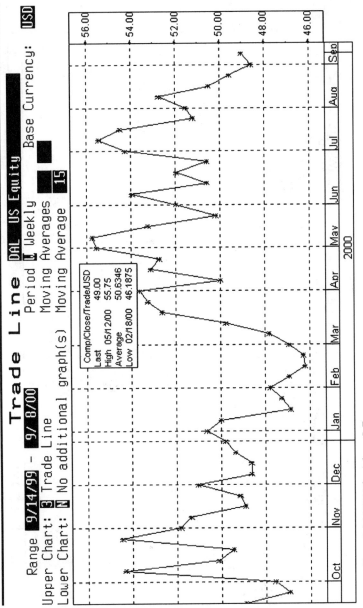

SOURCE: Copyright 2000 Bloomberg L.P.

Exhibit 6-6c United Airlines (UAL) Stock Prices

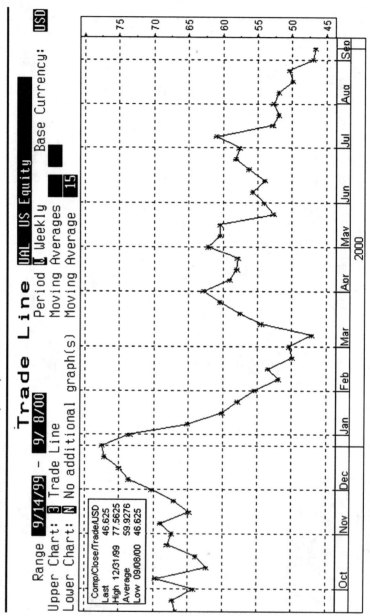

SOURCE: Copyright 2000 Bloomberg L.P.

Exhibit 6-6d Heating Oil Prices

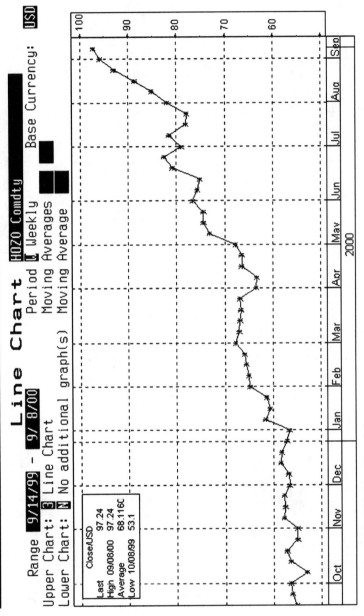

SOURCE: Copyright 2000 Bloomberg L.P.

Exhibit 6-7 Heating Oil Prices and Volatilities

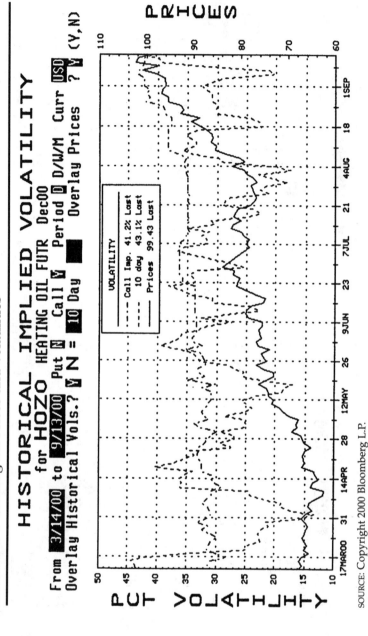

SOURCE: Copyright 2000 Bloomberg L.P.

Exhibit 6-8 Heating Oil
Price Potential

Sept 5 to Nov 1: 57 days

$365/57 = 6.40$

$\sqrt{6.40} = 2.53$

$0.4245/2.53 = 0.1678$

$96.35 \times 0.1678 = 16.17$

$96.35 + 16.17 = 112.52$

$96.35 - 16.17 = 80.18$

Developing a Sense of How Far Down *Down* Might Be

The next step in the decision process is to see what kinds of ranges are possible for the three stock prices in terms of the same 57-day period. Exhibit 6-9 shows these volatility-based estimates.

The question remains as to how likely stock price moves of these magnitudes might be. Here, option deltas can offer some guidance, even though the listed options on these stocks do not trade at strike prices that exactly match the low ends of the price ranges. For example, ABF puts are available with strike prices of 12.5 and 10. DAL and UAL puts are available with strike prices of 45 and 40.

To gauge the probabilities of prices moving lower, it makes sense to use the deltas of put options because out-of-the-money strike prices for puts are the ones below the current market level. Thus, with DAL stock trading at 48.25 per share, the next two lower strike prices are the 45 and 40 prices. Also, market convention signs deltas. Call deltas are listed as positive values. Put deltas are listed as negative values. For the purposes of this discussion, the signs have no importance.

Exhibit 6-10 shows the deltas of these options at both the higher and lower strike prices.

Recall that the delta of an option price estimates the probability that the option will expire in the money. That is, the 0.33 delta of the UAL 45 put indicates a 33 percent probability that the stock price will trade to a level at least slightly below (for a call, it would be slightly above) the strike price at option expiration.

Exhibit 6-9 Airline Stock Price Potential

	Current price	Implied volatility	Price range (68% probability) High	Low
ABF	14	38.33	16.12	11.88
DAL	48.25	36.28	55.17	41.33
UAL	46.75	26.22	51.59	41.91

DATA SOURCE: Bloomberg L.P.

Exhibit 6-10 Deltas Provide Downside Probabilities

	Higher strike deltas	Lower strike deltas
ABF	0.19	0.01
DAL	0.26	0.07
UAL	0.33	0.06

DATA SOURCE: Bloomberg L.P.

Based on current conditions, these deltas give no odds that the lower bounds of the three stock prices will be reached by the beginning of November. Conditions can change, of course. And the condition most likely to change, and most likely to have a strong impact on these stock prices, is the price of fuel.

Tying Stock Prices to Oil Prices

A number of quote services allow you to do regression analyses that show how two factors relate. A commonly performed regression relates the performance of a single stock to an index such as the Standard and Poor's (S&P) 500. Lacking access to such a quote service, your broker may be willing to help you with this kind of thing. A regression of United Airlines stock prices and December 2000 heating oil futures produces a graphic plot like the one shown in Exhibit 6-11.

For convenience, Exhibit 6-12 lists the key statistical results of similar regressions of all three airline stocks with heating oil futures and includes that day's stock prices.

Exhibit 6-11 Heating Oil–Stock Price Regressions (Bloomberg Scatter Plot)

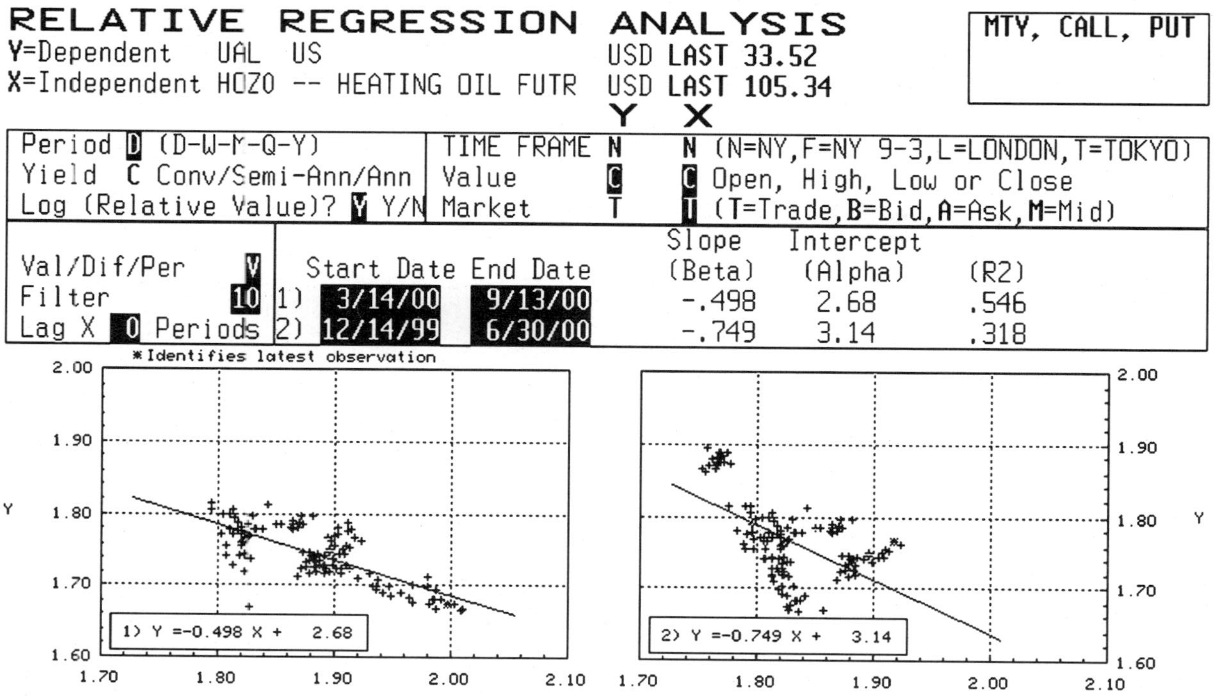
RELATIVE REGRESSION ANALYSIS
MTY, CALL, PUT
Y=Dependent UAL US USD LAST 33.52
X=Independent HOZ0 -- HEATING OIL FUTR USD LAST 105.34
Y X
Period D (D-W-M-Q-Y)
Yield C Conv/Semi-Ann/Ann
Log (Relative Value)? Y Y/N
TIME FRAME N N (N=NY,F=NY 9-3,L=LONDON,T=TOKYO)
Value C C Open, High, Low or Close
Market T T (T=Trade,B=Bid,A=Ask,M=Mid)
Val/Dif/Per V
Filter 10
Lag X 0 Periods
Start Date End Date
Slope (Beta)
Intercept (Alpha)
(R2)
1) 3/14/00 9/13/00 -.498 2.68 .546
2) 12/14/99 6/30/00 -.749 3.14 .318
* Identifies latest observation
Y
2.00
1.90
1.80
1.70
1.60
1.70
1.80
1.90
2.00
2.10
1) Y =-0.498 X + 2.68
2) Y =-0.749 X + 3.14

SOURCE: Copyright 2001 Bloomberg L.P.

Exhibit 6-12 Key Regression Statistics

	Price	Slope (beta)	R^2
ABF	14	−0.99	0.67
DAL	48.25	−0.17	0.23
UAL	46.75	−0.61	0.48

DATA SOURCE: Bloomberg L.P.

The slope statistic describes the slope of the line drawn through the scatter plot. The minus sign tells you that this is an inverse relationship. If oil prices move up, the stock price moves down. The value estimates the sensitivity of the stock price to a change in the oil price. You can see that during the period of the study, ABF moved virtually one-for-one with heating oil. DAL didn't seem especially sensitive, and UAL prices were very responsive to oil price changes.

The R^2 statistic indicates that, in the case of UAL, for example, the variation in the price of heating oil futures is capable of explaining 48 percent of the variation in the price of UAL stock.

The trouble with regressions is that they look at history, which may or may not have predictive power. And the regressions used here include only 6 months of data, which is a very short time. Still, the 6 months from early March through early September 2000 constituted a period of severe oil price increases, and all who use gasoline or fuel oils were lamenting the situation. As a result, these data do seem to describe what was going on in these markets.

What the Markets Suggest

From the looks of these statistics, it hardly seems worthwhile to put off buying Delta Airlines stock in hopes that the price will fall farther. The R^2 of 0.23 suggests that only 23 percent of the price variation in that stock is the result of the variation in heating oil prices. Combined with the 27 percent probability that you'll see $1.12 heating oil by the beginning of November, this seems like long odds against anything good happening in this case.

The situations with United Airlines and Airborne Freight may be different. In these cases, oil price change accounts for far more of the change in the stock price, and the slope statistics for these two stocks indicate far greater sensitivity to oil price change. With this in mind, you might decide that these stocks have some downside potential left and that it would be worth it to wait as much as 2 months to see what develops.

A Word of Caution

Notice that saying that the variation in the price of heating oil futures is capable of explaining 48 percent of the variation in the price of United Airlines stock is not at all to say that oil price change causes airline stock prices to change. These statistics do not claim this. If you look at the relevant price charts, you can see that heating oil prices and the prices of these stocks do vary inversely to some degree. The statistics are merely an attempt to help you put your intuitive grasp to work.

7

Futures Price Relationships Enrich the Story

The discussions of fed funds futures and the various yield curves indicate that interesting and helpful as it may be to keep track of the level of the fed funds rate or the yield on the 10-year Treasury note, the relationship between the two, and the way that relationship changes, may contain even more information than the yield levels themselves.

The same can be said of commodity prices, but not just prices alone. The central tenet of technical analysis is that the price of a futures contract or stock, or at least an historical record of these prices, contains "all ye know on earth and all ye need to know." Granted, prices do encapsulate a great deal of information. The very process of bid and offer give and take in a marketplace ensures this. Yet the act of distillation can obscure much that is interesting and important. Perhaps this is what prompted a veteran of the grain trade to state, categorically, "Price has no history." This may be going too far in the other direction.

Interesting as a price chart can be, though, relationships among futures delivery months typically tell a far richer story than prices in isolation, even a chart of them. Much as a yield curve describes the term structure of interest rates (the way yields vary at different maturities), so the contract-month-to-contract-month commodity prices, or spreads, define a kind of term structure for the given commodity.

Along with these spreads, commodity analysts often track the relationship between the prices of the actual commodity and the price of futures on that commodity. Like the spread relationships, this cash-futures price relationship, called the *basis*, is typically far more predictable than the price in isolation.

In fact, the seasonal basis and spread patterns operate quite independently of the level of prices. When the patterns depart from the norm, this is a sign that all is not well. Investors should heed this sign and begin looking for reasons and thinking about how to adapt their investment strategies to the new situation.

The Basis

Basis is one of many financial market terms that mean different things in different contexts. You've seen the term *basis point* used to indicate ⅟₁₀₀ of a percentage point. Another use of the term originated in the grain trade but applies equally well to all cash-futures relationships.

For the physical commodities, the basis calculation is simple. The cash price minus the futures price equals the basis. Consider the basis for corn, copper, heating oil, and 10-year Treasury notes, with readings taken on August 30, 2000 and October 10, 2000, as shown in Exhibit 7-1.

The corn price is quoted in cents and quarters of a cent per bushel. In this example, 155 amounts to $1.55 per bushel. Copper is

Exhibit 7-1 The Bases for Physical Commodities

Commodity	Cash	Futures	Basis
	8/30/00		
Corn	155½	193¾	−38¼
Copper	0.8850	0.8970	−0.0120
Heating Oil	0.9918	0.9707	0.0211
	10/10/00		
Corn	177½	203½	−26
Copper	0.9025	0.9055	−0.0030
Heating Oil	0.9944	0.9976	−0.0032

quoted in cents per pound, here converted to dollars. A quote of 0.8850 amounts to 88.5 cents per pound. Heating oil is quoted in cents per gallon, again converted to dollars. A quote of 0.9918 amounts to 99.18 cents per gallon. You can see that, for the physical commodities, the basis can have a positive or a negative value.

Calculating the basis for Treasury-note futures is slightly more complicated. Eight Treasury notes with quite different characteristics are eligible for delivery into the futures contract, the number at any moment depending on how many issues qualify in terms of a specified range of maturities. To make them comparable, the Chicago Board of Trade (CBOT) devised a conversion factor system that essentially prices them to yield 6 percent. To calculate a Treasury-note basis for a given security, you multiply that security's conversion factor by the futures price and subtract that product from the cash security price. Treasury-note basis is typically quoted in thirty-seconds, so a basis of 5.8 denotes $5.8/32$.

For example, with the 6⅛ percent of August 07 trading at 101-13 (or 101.4063) and having a 1.0066 conversion factor and the December 10-year Treasury-note futures trading at 100-18 (or 100.5625), the basis is 5.8.

Cash price – (futures price × conversion factor) = basis

$$101.4063 - (100.5625 \times 1.0066) = 0.1801$$

$$0.1801 \times 32 = 5.76 \text{ (round to 5.8)}$$

The Force of Arbitrage

Keep in mind that at futures delivery, the cash and futures prices must converge. The basis must be zero. Suppose that copper futures reached 92 cents at futures delivery, but actual copper was trading at 93 cents. The futures contract specifies delivery of 25,000 lb. This means that an arbitrager could go long futures and take delivery of 25,000 lb of copper (the amount in one contract) at a cost of $23,000 (25,000 × $0.92 = $23,000). He or she could immediately sell it for 93 cents a pound, or $23,250 (25,000 × $0.93 = $23,250), and earn a risk-free return of $250. Done in size, this could be worthwhile.

Beguiling as the prospect of a risk-free return may seem, arbitrage is rather like some of the ads you see on TV—you know, where a driver can do wonderful and exciting things because he or she is in a special car or using special tires, but a print message appears at the bottom of the screen to the effect that this was done by a professional stunt driver and should not be tried at home with the family car.

Suffice it to say that the financial equivalents of the professional stunt drivers do pounce on arbitrage opportunities as they emerge. Their buying of futures will tend to drive the futures price higher. Their selling of the actual copper will tend to drive that price lower. The arbitragers will keep doing this until the trade is no longer profitable. The end result is that arbitrage activity forces the cash and futures prices into alignment in a very short time. This makes futures prices extremely trustworthy.

Of course, convergence only happens at delivery. At other times, the cash and futures prices can be fairly far apart. Yet the basis defines what this relationship should be. Take the case of the 10-year Treasury note. The basis of a Treasury security has two components.

The larger, referred to as *carry*, consists of the difference between the interest income the security pays and the cost of a fully financed position in the security for the number of days to futures delivery. Treasury securities pay interest (make coupon payments) twice a year. These coupon periods vary from security to security and from year to year, but consider the case of the $6\frac{1}{8}$ percent of August 07. To see what the coupon payment would be 90 days from futures delivery, you solve for

$$\text{Coupon}/2 \times \text{days}/184 = \text{interest income}$$

$$6.125/2 \times 90/184 = 1.4980$$

The financing cost factors together the full price of the security, the financing rate, and a day count. Omitting detail, suppose that the interest payments and the financing costs at 90-day intervals are those shown in Exhibit 7-2. You can see that, all else the same, these payments decline in regular increments as delivery approaches.

Exhibit 7-2 Carry Across Time

Day to delivery	Interest payment	Financing cost	Carry
90	1.4980	1.4690	0.0290
60	0.9986	0.9793	0.0193
30	0.4993	0.4897	0.0096

The other, smaller piece of the Treasury-note basis is the value of the seller's delivery options. In a delivery situation, the short, or futures seller, gets to choose which of the eight eligible securities to deliver and when in the delivery month to deliver them. These delivery options can be valued much as can other options. What matters here is not how this is done. The fixed-income pros can take care of this. Suffice it to say that, all else the same, an option with 90 days to expiration is worth more than one with 60 days to expiration, and the 60-day option will be worth more than one with 30 days to expiration. And, at expiration, an at-the-money option will be valueless.

The schematic diagram of Exhibit 7-3 captures the key points of the behavior of the basis of a Treasury security. In reality, the spot price will bounce around as yields change. The financing rate can change, as can the option values. Still, at any moment, these factors make it possible to define fair value. Any time the two prices drift away from this, arbitrage is possible—just as it is with copper, heating oil, corn, or any other commodity for which a futures market exists. As it does at delivery, this arbitrage activity drives prices back into alignment.

Commodity Spreads

Futures price spreads generate the same signals as the basis and are more readily available on the *Wall Street Journal* futures page or on any quote screen. Soybeans, for example, trade on a January, March, May, July, August, September, November cycle, while crude oil, unleaded gasoline, heating oil, and copper trade on a monthly cycle. Had you looked under the "Settlement" column on the November 5, 1998 quote page, you would have seen the array of Exhibit 7-4 for the soybean market.

Keep in mind that the January price of 567.50 (the 567 here is cents per bushel) is the November 5 price for next January delivery. This is worth emphasizing. It is not a prediction of what the price will be in January. It is the price a buyer is willing to pay *today* for a specified future delivery.

In this case, notice that the prices go up between 8 and 8.5 cents at a time. For crops such as corn and soybeans, it costs between 5 and 6 cents per bushel per month to store and finance inventory,

Exhibit 7-3 A Bond Basis Schematic

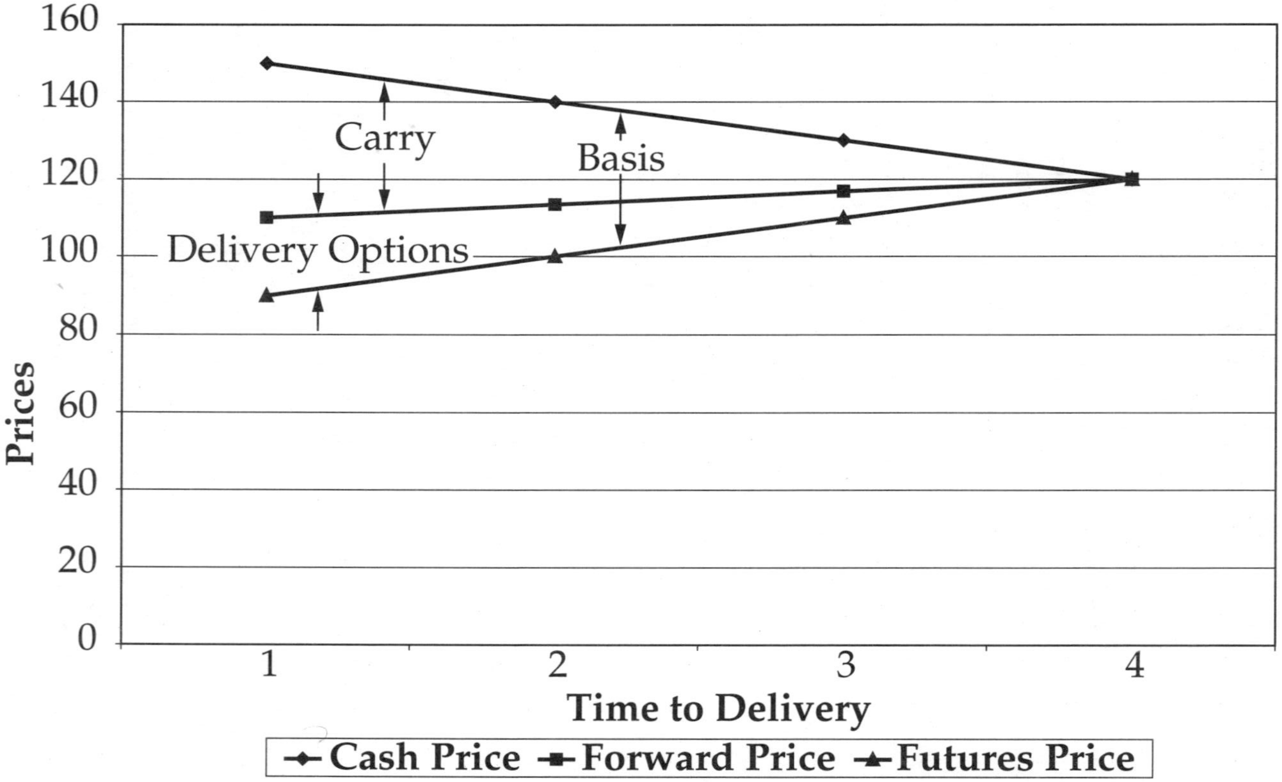

Prices

160
140
120
100
80
60
40
20
0

Carry

Basis

Delivery Options

1 2 3 4

Time to Delivery

→ Cash Price → Forward Price → Futures Price

Exhibit 7-4 Positive
Spreads Reward Storage

	Price	Spread
Nov	559.50	—
Jan	567.50	8.00
Mar	576.00	8.50
May	584.25	8.25
Jul	592.75	8.50

depending on the level of interest rates. This, in market jargon, is the *full cost of carry*, or just *carry*. Seldom will the market pay full carry. Never will it pay more than that. The January price means that the market will pay producers or merchants the spot price (the price for delivery immediately, or on the spot) plus about 80 percent of carry.

Think about why the market might be willing to pay more for deferred delivery. In early November, with the harvest just ended, supplies should be plentiful. Users do not especially need soybeans and want producers and merchants to store this crop against later need. These prices are the market's way of telling the producers this. The message is that if they store the beans, the market will pay as much as 80 percent of the cost of storage. This is reward enough to drive beans into the silos.

The soybean situation in early June of 1998 looked very different. Then you would have seen the spreads shown in Exhibit 7-5. These spreads are strongly negative. The July-August spread is roughly double full carry. The August-September spread is more than triple. Even though the market will never pay more than full carry when the spreads are positive, it will penalize storage far more strongly. There is no limit on how negative the spreads can be.

This makes sense in terms of where June is in the crop year. The old crop should be pretty well used up by that time. The new crop will not be available until late September or October, or even later. Here, the market needs more soybeans than are easily available and must find a way to draw them out of storage. This often takes extra motivation, in the form of pricing. In effect, the market is saying it will pay almost 20 cents per bushel more for July delivery

Exhibit 7-5 Negative
Spreads Penalize Storage

	Price	Spread
Jul	616.25	—
Aug	605.25	–11.00
Sep	586.50	–18.75
Nov	582.25	–4.25
Jan	588.75	6.50

than for September delivery. Notice, too, that the positive
November-January spread shows that the market is already pricing in some carry for the new crop.

A Sense of History

These spreads provide far more reliable information than prices
alone, although at extreme prices in either direction other factors
come into play. Exhibit 7-6 takes some work to understand, but it
contains a wealth of information about the kinds of signals these
markets can generate, in this case about the soybean market.

Each gray dot represents the first delivery day of an expiring
contract. The line extending out from the dot shows the directions
of the spreads going forward from that point. If the line heads up,
the spreads are in some degree like the ones in Exhibit 7-4. If the
line goes down, the spreads are more or less like those in Exhibit
7-5. You can see that the lines change direction, when they do, at
the intersections between price levels on the vertical axis and contract month designations on the horizontal axis. Notice the line that
starts in the Sep-95 column at roughly 620 per bushel (the dot has
been replaced by a star to help you locate it). This line shows positive spreads until the Jul-96 contract and then inverts (heads down)
for several months. You can see a strong seasonal pattern in all the
lines between 550 and 800 per bushel. All the lines reflect the pattern of this first line in kind if not in degree.

But look at the line that starts at the intersection of the 880 price
and the Jul-97 contract (the dot has been replaced by a square). This

Exhibit 7-6 Soybean Price Curve

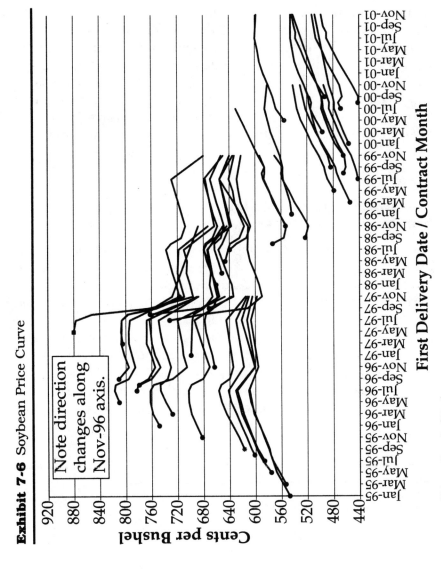

SOURCE: Chicago Board of Trade

113

line drops precipitously for several months. When crop prices get this high, it isn't usually because demand is so strong. Rather, it's because there's little to sell. A drought or too much rain at the wrong time caused a short crop, and the market is telling the producers that, with so little to sell, they'd better not store it.

Conversely, the spreads at the bottom right are all positive, even though they extend across the time of the year when you might expect to see a storage signal. Prices this low usually follow large crops and plentiful carryover from years before. With all those beans spilling out of the bins, the need to attract scarce goods simply never developed. Sellers needed to move them and didn't need any special coaxing.

The Energy Markets Signal Similar Storage Messages

The futures price spreads work the same way in other physical markets. Exhibit 7-7 shows the spreads for unleaded gasoline futures at intervals during the summer of 2000.

This market was practically screaming, "Don't store." What the late July spreads say is that the market would pay 18.78 cents per gallon more for delivery in August than it would for delivery in November. (To derive this 18.78 cents, add the spreads in the column following the 7/28/00 prices: −10.03 + −6.15 + −2.60 = −18.78.) The market wanted all the gasoline it could get its hands on—and right away. Looked at the other way, this is a huge penalty for stor-

Exhibit 7-7 An Antistorage Imperative in Gasoline

Contract month	6/28/00	Spread	7/28/00	Spread
Jul	103.44	—	—	—
Aug	99.91	−3.53	95.03	—
Sep	94.01	−5.90	85.00	−10.03
Oct	86.51	−7.50	78.85	−6.15
Nov	81.91	−4.60	76.25	−2.60

DATA SOURCE: Bloomberg L.P.

age. The situation the market was dealing with involved scant supplies and huge demand. A big part of the problem, of course, was that U.S. refineries were operating full-bore and couldn't produce more if they wanted to. These spreads were the result.

Spreads such as these can help you look into the near future, if you have a grasp of the normal patterns. When you do, you can often spot problems developing earlier than most people do, including people getting paid to know what's going on. Your investment strategies can benefit accordingly.

Heating oil futures offer a case in point, based on the spreads for 1998, 1999, and 2000 that are shown in Exhibit 7-8. Carry in heating oil and unleaded gasoline is close to 2 cents per gallon per month, again depending on interest rates. The May through August spreads for 1998 show a market that was rewarding storage. The July spreads, for example, represent between 70 and 80 percent of carry. The market was saying, with these spreads, that it didn't need heating oil at present and would help pay for storage. This makes sense in the middle of summer. The pricing structure during the summer and fall months encourages the buildup of stocks against winter needs. Notice that in the last three months of 1998 the spreads narrowed considerably. The storage signal was weakening.

The 1999 spreads offer quite a contrast. The June, July, and August spreads are much narrower than the 1998 spreads in the same months. These 1999 markets are paying no more than 40 percent of carry, not nearly enough to motivate storage. By November and December, the spreads were all negative. The market wanted all the heating oil it could get its hands on—now. Many of these November and December spreads exceed full carry. Recall that when the market inverts (oil and metal people use the word "backwardation" to indicate negative spreads like these), there is no economic limit on how wide the spreads can be. The full carry limit only applies to positive spreads.

The spreads for 2000 are even more interesting. For one thing, the spreads are huge—multiples of full carry. In no month are all the spreads positive. In June and July, when you would expect stock building to begin, even the spreads that are positive are barely so. These spreads offer no storage imperative. By August, the market is again inverted—not as sharply as earlier, but any inversion at this time of year is remarkable.

Exhibit 7-8 Heating Oil Futures Spreads

Heat	1/28/98		2/27/98		3/30/98		4/29/98		5/29/98		6/29/98	
Feb	47.76											
Mar	48.24	0.48	42.80									
Apr	48.64	0.40	43.46	0.66	44.18							
May	49.04	0.40	44.01	0.55	44.74	0.56	43.08					
Jun	49.34	0.30	44.71	0.70	45.34	0.60	43.64	0.56	39.10			
Jul	49.84	0.50	45.51	0.80	46.14	0.80	44.39	0.75	40.37	1.27	38.55	
Aug	50.54	0.70	46.41	0.90	47.04	0.90	45.39	1.00	41.67	1.30	39.34	0.79
Sep			47.41	1.00	48.04	1.00	46.39	1.00	43.12	1.45	40.54	1.20
Oct					49.04	1.00	47.34	0.95	44.52	1.40	41.99	1.45
Nov							48.34	1.00	45.82	1.30	43.44	1.45
Dec									47.12	1.30	44.79	1.35
Jan											45.79	1.00
Feb												
Mar												
Apr												
May												
Jun												
Jul												

Heat	1/28/99		2/26/99		3/29/99		4/29/99		5/28/99		6/28/99	
Feb	32.55											
Mar	32.81	0.26	32.29									
Apr	33.21	0.40	32.37	0.08	43.20							
May	33.76	0.55	32.87	0.50	43.26	0.06	44.79					
Jun	34.51	0.75	33.42	0.55	43.36	0.10	45.11	0.32	39.43			
Jul	35.36	0.85	34.07	0.65	43.66	0.30	45.46	0.35	39.63	0.20	45.02	
Aug	36.16	0.80	34.82	0.75	44.16	0.50	45.91	0.45	40.43	0.80	45.69	0.67
Sep			35.67	0.85	44.76	0.60	46.51	0.60	41.43	1.00	46.49	0.80
Oct					45.41	0.65	47.11	0.60	42.33	0.90	47.29	0.80
Nov							47.61	0.50	43.18	0.85	47.99	0.70
Dec									43.98	0.80	48.69	0.70
Jan												
Feb												
Mar												
Apr												
May												
Jun												
Jul												

Heat	1/28/00		2/28/00		3/28/00		4/28/00		5/26/00		6/28/00	
Feb	92.51											
Mar	73.27	-19.24	81.67									
Apr	68.07	-5.20	75.81	-5.86	74.16							
May	64.87	-3.20	71.01	-4.80	68.16	-6.00	73.18					
Jun	62.57	-2.30	68.06	-2.95	65.56	-2.60	67.19	-5.99	76.39			
Jul	61.12	-1.45	66.56	-1.50	64.46	-1.10	65.39	-1.80	74.28	-2.11	81.59	
Aug	60.42	-0.70	65.66	-0.90	64.26	-0.20	65.14	-0.25	73.93	-0.35	81.68	0.09
Sep			65.76	0.10	64.76	0.50	65.59	0.45	74.03	0.10	81.83	0.15
Oct					65.16	0.40	65.99	0.40	74.18	0.15	81.93	0.10
Nov							66.29	0.30	74.33	0.15	81.78	-0.15
Dec									74.33	0.00	81.43	-0.35
Jan												
Feb												
Mar												

DATA SOURCE: Bloomberg L.P.

7/28/98		8/28/98		9/28/98		10/29/98		11/30/98		12/28/98	
35.99											
37.37	1.38	34.97									
38.87	1.50	35.74	0.77	41.73							
40.47	1.60	36.99	1.25	42.95	1.22	38.36					
42.07	1.60	38.49	1.50	44.05	1.10	39.47	1.11	31.32			
43.22	1.15	39.84	1.35	45.00	0.95	40.62	1.15	32.13	0.81	32.51	
44.02	0.80	40.89	1.05	45.65	0.65	41.42	0.80	33.21	1.08	33.31	0.80
		41.44	0.55	45.80	0.15	41.77	0.35	34.06	0.85	33.86	0.55
				45.70	-0.10	41.82	0.05	34.76	0.70	34.26	0.40
						41.97	0.15	35.51	0.75	34.71	0.45
								36.26	0.75	35.36	0.65
										36.11	0.75

7/27/99		8/27/99		9/27/99		10/28/99		11/29/99		12/29/99	
50.71											
51.55	0.84	55.99									
52.35	0.80	56.64	0.65	62.12							
53.10	0.75	57.29	0.65	62.70	0.58	57.70					
53.75	0.65	57.84	0.55	63.20	0.50	58.16	0.46	67.13			
54.05	0.30	57.99	0.15	63.25	0.05	58.41	0.25	66.94	-0.19	70.41	
				62.45	-0.80	58.21	-0.20	65.64	-1.30	69.77	-0.64
				60.20	-2.25	57.21	-1.00	63.54	-2.10	67.27	-2.50
						55.56	-1.65	60.74	-2.80	64.47	-2.80
						53.91	-1.65	57.99	-2.75	61.52	-2.95
								56.19	-1.80	59.32	-2.20
										58.12	-1.20

7/28/00		8/28/00		9/26/00	
76.77					
76.91	0.14	99.88			
77.31	0.40	99.25	-0.63	92.85	
77.66	0.35	96.97	-2.28	93.15	0.30
77.86	0.20	95.47	-1.50	93.10	-0.05
77.51	-0.35	93.47	-2.00	92.60	-0.50
		90.07	-3.40	90.60	-2.00
				86.80	-3.80

Consider what you know about the year 2000, as far as the gasoline and oil markets are concerned. During late spring and early summer, high gasoline and diesel fuel prices were front-page news in many parts of the country. Members of Congress were talking about holding hearings to find out why this should be so. In Europe, people faced even higher prices and more severe shortages. The media carried pictures of protest demonstrations and long lines of frustrated motorists. Whether to release some fraction of U.S. strategic oil reserves became a minor talking point between U.S. presidential candidates.

In short, the summer of 2000 was not a normal one in the energy markets. Refined products were scarce, relative to demand, and the 2000 spreads reflect this. What is germane here is not whether OPEC is the culprit or the lack of adequate refining capacity is. Rather, a study of these spreads suggests that the markets were sending up signal flares that all was not well as early as the summer of 1999. Seeing signals like these should alert investors to dig deeper in their search for understanding.

As an investor, you may not need to know exactly what is causing changes in these spreads—at least not immediately. It may suffice to know that transportation companies may suffer when they cannot pass these rising costs to consumers. Because petroleum is an important feedstock for a variety of plastics and chemicals, companies in these sectors could also feel the stress of a tight oil supply situation and the resulting higher input prices.

It follows that if you were a holder of stocks in these sectors and had noticed the spreads narrowing in the summer of 1999, it might have been a good time to consider taking defensive action. By the time the disappointing earnings reports come out, it may be too late.

Gauging the Profitability of Refining

Another kind of futures spread can take your search for answers about energy another step further. The presence of crude oil, unleaded gasoline, and heating oil futures allows you "to build a paper refinery," as futures people say. Certainly, paper barrels are easier to handle than wet ones. The idea is that refiners acquire crude oil at one end of the refining process, add value through the refining process, and ship the refined products out at the other end, at a gross margin that reflects the addition of value.

A common version of this refining spread balances three barrels of crude oil against two barrels of gasoline and one of heating oil. This approximates the ratio of light and medium distillates in an average barrel yield. The formula to solve is

$$\{[(2 \times gas) + heat] - [3(crude/42)]\}/3 = \text{gross margin}$$

The terms *gas*, *heat*, and *crude* represent the futures prices for those three contracts for a given delivery month, and the divisor of 42 reflects the fact that a barrel contains 42 gallons. The gross margin, then, is expressed in cents per gallon but can be converted to dollars per barrel by multiplying by 42.

Every refinery has a different breakeven level, but a good ballpark figure is 4 cents per gallon, or $1.68 per barrel. Exhibit 7-9 shows refining spread calculations for the summers of 1998, 1999, and 2000.

In Exhibit 7-9, the "Contract" column shows the nearest crude oil delivery month trading on the specified date. This late in May, this is the July contract, and so on. The "Gas" and "Heat" columns

Exhibit 7-9 Comparing Refining Spreads

Contract		Gas	Heat	Crude	Gross Margin	
					Cents/Gal	$/Barrel
5/28/98	Jul	0.5007	0.4037	14.85	0.1148	4.82
6/29/98	Aug	0.4704	0.3934	14.07	0.1097	4.61
7/29/98	Sep	0.4345	0.3737	14.22	0.0757	3.18
8/27/98	Oct	0.3984	0.3574	13.23	0.0697	2.93
9/28/98	Nov	0.4589	0.4295	15.64	0.0767	3.22
5/28/99	Jul	0.5031	0.3963	16.84	0.0665	2.79
6/28/99	Aug	0.5314	0.4569	18.23	0.0725	3.05
7/27/99	Sep	0.6179	0.5155	20.38	0.0985	4.14
8/27/99	Oct	0.6296	0.5664	21.27	0.1021	4.29
9/27/99	Nov	0.6930	0.6270	24.61	0.0850	3.57
5/26/00	Jul	0.9659	0.7428	30.00	0.1772	7.44
6/28/00	Aug	0.9991	0.8168	32.06	0.1750	7.35
7/28/00	Sep	0.8500	0.7691	28.02	0.1559	6.55
8/28/00	Oct	0.9093	0.9925	32.87	0.1544	6.48
9/26/00	Nov	0.8920	0.9315	31.87	0.1464	6.15

Note: A ballpark breakeven is $1.68/barrel.

DATA SOURCE: Bloomberg L.P.

show prices in dollars per gallon. The "Crude" column shows prices in dollars per barrel. Under "Gross Margin," the "Cents/Gal" column uses the formula discussed above to calculate the refining margin and expresses it in dollars per gallon. Recall that a ballpark breakeven is 0.04, or 4 cents per gallon. Finally, the "$/Barrel" column multiplies the "Cents/Gal" result by 42 to convert to dollars per barrel.

You can see that all these spreads (most of them well more than double breakeven) indicate that refining was profitable. During the summer of 2000, refining spreads soared. In percentage terms, these gross margins increased considerably more than the price of crude oil.

An old futures market saying is that the best cure for high prices is high prices. The best cure for low prices is low prices. Logic suggests that when an activity is profitable, people will want to do a lot of it. It follows that if the refining margin is approaching 4 or 4½ times breakeven, refiners should be stepping up production to take advantage of this opportunity. This increased production should shift the supply-demand balance enough to cause prices to start coming down, even with relatively higher crude oil prices.

Prices haven't come down, though. This suggests that the trouble may be that refiners cannot increase production any more than they already have. Indeed, by late summer 2000, U.S. refineries were operating at around 95 percent capacity. The common wisdom holds that 85 percent is a comfortable full capacity. Above this level, the risk of breakdowns and environmental problems escalates. This makes it at least plausible to conclude that OPEC may not be quite the culprit people like to think it is and that U.S. refining capacity may be more of an issue here.

The Time to Act

In all these cases, it should be clear that relationships tell a richer story than prices alone. It should also be clear that these prices do not tell you everything there is to know. They can be likened to the messenger—as in don't kill the. . . . When something untoward happens in the spreads, when they violate the normal patterns, this should prompt you to look for more information. Above all, such signals should prompt consideration of your investment strategies.

You should be asking whether this is a time to shift assets from one sector to another, whether you should sit out the next few dances, or whether it's time to move aggressively into a sector that hasn't looked too promising in the recent past.

The "What's News" column of a recent *Wall Street Journal* carried two items offering cases in point. The first reported, "ExxonMobil, Chevron, and Texaco reported record earnings for the third quarter amid soaring prices for oil and natural gas, exceeding expectations." The second item reported, "Railroad companies Burlington Northern and CSX posted lackluster quarterly results, reflecting rising fuel costs and disappointing revenue." Of course, this is hardly the time to move on stocks such as these. The time would have been a year or more before these items emerged when you could have shifted from the stock of a company, such as one of the railroads, that was likely to have trouble going forward and into the stock of one that could benefit from these wildly profitable refining margins.

The situation with oil products in 1999 and 2000 is only one example of this kind of thing. Similar stories unfold in all the commodities futures markets. Often, though not always, the plot line starts to develop early enough to prompt action when it will do some good.

8

Commodity Prices—
The Next Link
in the Chain

Industrial commodity prices often signal economic shifts well in advance of other signals. The reason for this is not hard to find.

Manufacturers preparing for an anticipated upturn in demand for their output must buy raw commodities such as copper, aluminum, or steel early in the process. This is not just an upstream decision. It takes place close to where the stream comes bubbling out of the earth.

Next, if manufacturers of plumbing supplies, heating and air-conditioning equipment, and automotive components all start competing for available supplies of these metals, you can expect to see rising prices in these commodities well in advance of signs of activity from the housing or automotive sectors.

The Trouble with
Commodity Indexes

Several groups have put together commodity price indexes to provide investors with one number to keep track of, much as a stock index provides one number with which to gauge the activity of a large and complex market. Not all these indexes prove as useful as you might think they should. To see why, consider three well-known commodity price indexes: the Bridge/CRB Futures Index (CRB), the Goldman Sachs Commodity Index (GSCI), and the

Journal of Commerce–Economic Cycle Research Institute Industrial Price Index (JOC-ECRI IPI).

The first thing you notice when you look at these indexes is that not all commodity indexes are created equal. Checking the broad categories of Exhibit 8-1 (which may not total exactly 100 percent due to rounding error), you can see that while 67.50 percent of the GSCI consists of energy market commodities, only 17.6 and 16.65 percent of the CRB and JOC-ECRI IPI, respectively, are energy market commodities. Notice, too, that the JOC-ECRI IPI gives far more weight to industrial metals than either of the other two indexes, and it completely omits agricultural commodities.

Within the broad categories, these indexes get even more various. To begin with, the JOC-ECRI IPI omits all agricultural commodities (subcategorized in Exhibit 8-1 as grains, livestock, and "softs," although you could argue that burlap, cotton, hides, and tallow are agricultural because they come from plants or animals). The CRB and the GSCI include almost the same commodities, but the CRB distinguishes between grains and softs (cocoa, coffee, orange juice, and sugar), while the GSCI lumps them all together. Further, the GSCI includes cotton in this category, where the CRB calls it an industrial and the JOC-ECRI IPI has a separate textiles category.

The metals categories are vastly different as well. The CRB and the GSCI include precious metals, while the JOC-ECRI IPI does not. The CRB includes only copper in its industrials category, while the GSCI includes aluminum, copper, lead, nickel, tin, and zinc. The JOC-ECRI IPI adds steel to the six nonferrous metals.

Supply Shocks Can Blur Signals

These differences are worth focusing on because they cause these indexes to respond to economic events in rather different ways and to differ markedly when it comes to economic forecasting.

The energy and agricultural commodities are prone to huge supply shocks. Weather extremes in the U.S. grain belt can send grain prices soaring, but this tells you nothing about demand for these commodities. Typically, when grain prices reach record highs, it isn't because demand has escalated. Rather, the high prices mean

Exhibit 8-1 Comparing Commodity Indexes
(by Percentage Weights)

Index components	CRB (%)	GSCI (%)	JOC-ECRI IPI (%)
Energy	**17.6**	**67.50**	**16.65**
Brent Crude Oil	—	12.55	—
Crude Oil	5.9	27.02	5.55
Gas Oil	—	3.35	—
Heating Oil	5.9	8.29	—
Natural Gas	5.9	11.31	—
Unleaded Gasoline	—	4.98	—
Benzene	—	—	5.55
Ethylene	—	—	5.55
Base Metals	**5.9**	**6.69**	**38.85**
Aluminum	—	3.24	5.55
Copper	5.9	1.85	5.55
Lead	—	0.23	5.55
Nickel	—	0.58	5.55
Steel	—	—	5.55
Tin	—	0.09	5.55
Zinc	—	0.70	5.55
Grains	**17.7**	**9.77**	**—**
Corn	5.9	3.32	—
Soybeans	5.9	1.83	—
Wheat	5.9	3.32	—
Wheat (red)	—	1.30	—
Livestock	**11.8**	**8.11**	**—**
Lean Hogs	5.9	2.40	—
Live Cattle	5.9	5.71	—
Precious Metals	**17.6**	**2.02**	**—**
Gold	5.9	1.62	—
Platinum	5.9	0.21	—
Silver	5.9	0.19	—
Softs	**23.6**	**3.58**	**—**
Cocoa	5.9	0.18	—
Coffee	5.9	0.84	—
Orange Juice	5.9	0.52	—
Sugar	5.9	2.04	—
Textiles	**5.9**	**2.16**	**16.65**
Burlap	—	—	5.55
Cotton	5.9	2.16	5.55
Polyester	—	—	5.55
Miscellaneous	**—**	**—**	**27.75**
Hides	—	—	5.55
Plywood	—	—	5.55
Red Oak	—	—	5.55
Rubber	—	—	5.55
Tallow	—	—	5.55

DATA SOURCE: Economic Cycle Research Institute

that large numbers of producers have little or nothing to sell. Demand may be stable or changed, but the grain prices offer scant help when it comes to predicting anything about the overall state of the economy in the months ahead.

Oil prices tend to soar for supply-oriented reasons as well. The Iraqi invasion of Kuwait in 1990, for example, cut off the supply of crude oil from two significant sources and threatened further interruptions of supplies. This drove prices sharply higher, but the price increases had little or no forecasting value.

During the summer of 2000, crude oil and refined product prices soared again—in both the United States and Europe. Granted, the OPEC countries were trying to hold down production to generate more income for themselves. Still, this didn't seem to be the main problem. Rather, U.S. refiners were running full bore and simply couldn't produce enough refined products to achieve supply-demand balance. This kind of situation, again, creates enough noise to hopelessly distort the economic signals.

Notice that over 90 percent of the GSCI consists of commodities prone to supply shocks. Indeed, a regression analysis of the GSCI against crude oil futures shows an R^2 of 0.965. That is, price movements in crude oil account for roughly 97 percent of the change in the value of the GSCI.

A Demand-Driven Index
Seems a Better Forecaster

All things considered, then, the index, of these three, that seems most likely to be helpful is the JOC-ECRI IPI. Focused as it is on the raw materials that manufacturers use in abundance, especially the industrial metals, it should be able to signal the existence of the kinds of price pressures that lead to turns in the inflationary cycle well in advance of an actual turn. In fact, the lead is typically a matter of 10 or 11 months.

A look at Exhibit 8-2, which plots the JOC-ECRI IPI growth rate from the beginning of 1974 to 2000, seems to motivate this preference rather clearly. The shaded areas represent U.S. inflation cycle downturns—more commonly, recessions.

Taking a panoramic view, you can see that these industrial commodity prices peak during economic expansions and trough

Exhibit 8-2 JOC-ECRI IPI Growth Rate (%)

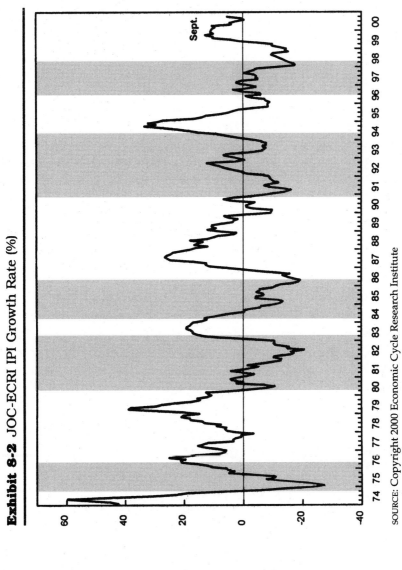

SOURCE: Copyright 2000 Economic Cycle Research Institute

during recessionary periods. Taking a closer look, you can see that an inflationary cycle downturn is preceded, in most cases, by a sharp commodity price downturn. Conversely, sharp upturns seem to lead most of the recoveries by at least a quarter or two.

The Economic Cycle Research Institute (ECRI) researchers use these data to generate another interesting insight. Exhibit 8-3 compares their "U.S. future inflation gauge" with the fed funds rate from 1987 to September 2000.

You can see that only one recessionary period (represented by the shaded area) mars this economic landscape. However, the Federal Reserve (Fed) has moved its fed funds target in increments large and small as it has adjusted the supply of credit flowing into the U.S. economy while striving to help the current expansion continue. A Fed policy shift, recall, shows up in the economic numbers roughly two quarters later.

This exhibit shows commodity prices to have consistently led changes in the fed funds rate by one or two quarters. Among other things, this chart motivates the ECRI claim that its index leads cycle changes by 10 or 11 months. The fed funds lag and the amount commodity prices change seem to lead fed funds falls consistently in this ballpark.

This is interesting because it means that keeping a weather eye on commodity prices can help you formulate a story about what is going on in the economy that might affect stocks in which you are interested well in advance of the issuance of earnings reports or other kinds of information.

Copper: Everyman's Economist

Economic folklore suggests that copper can serve as a useful economic indicator. It has even been claimed that copper "has a better economic forecasting record than most human beings." The idea of paying special attention to copper prices gains credibility from the facts that copper plays an important role in the manufacture of a broad range of goods and that the copper purchase must occur early in the process.

Exhibit 8-3 U.S. Future Inflation Gauge

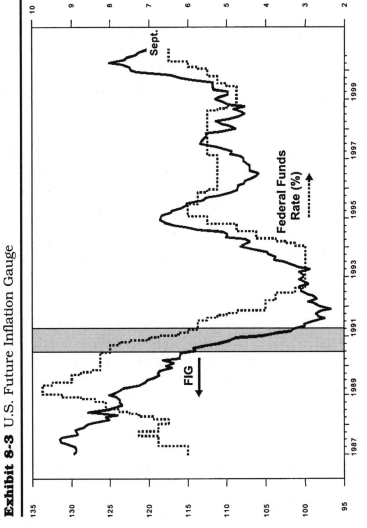

SOURCE: Copyright 2000 Economic Cycle Research Institute

Consequently, copper is ordinarily an excellent indicator of demand. Granted, strikes, political turmoil in mining regions, and mine disasters can cause supply problems that produce static in the message. Still, industrial demand is ordinarily the main driver of this market.

Apart from a simple tracking of copper prices, copper watchers have devised interesting ways of determining what is going on in this sensitive market. Two exchanges trade copper futures—the COMEX division of the New York Mercantile Exchange (NYMEX) and the London Metals Exchange (LME). As do any of the futures exchanges offering physical delivery contracts, these exchanges certify a number of warehouses as regular for delivery.

It should surprise no one that when demand for copper slacks off, copper prices drop, and the warehouses accumulate inventory. When industrial demand picks up, prices rise, and the stocks diminish. Exhibit 8-4 shows this relationship between copper prices and warehouse inventories for the period from 1981 through 1999.

The heavier line plots monthly average spot prices expressed in dollars per pound. The peak price on this chart occurred in late 1988, when copper traded close to $1.56 per pound. More recently, its price has sunk as low as $0.63 per pound.

The shaded area represents COMEX and LME warehouse stocks in thousands of short tons. A short ton is 2,000 lb. Most of the world markets trade in metric tons, which are equivalent to 1.102 short tons, or 2,204 lb. Market shorthand reserves the spelling *ton* for short ton and the spelling *tonne* for metric ton. The peak inventory during this period, reached in the second quarter of 1999, was 900 on the scale, or 900,000 short tons.

In "big picture" terms, you can see that the price peaks more or less mirror the inventory troughs. At times, but not always, price change seems to lead inventory change slightly. This seems logical enough.

A Look at the Futures Price Spreads

As is the case with fed funds, grain, and oil futures, the month-to-month relationships often tell a richer story than the prices themselves. The message is similar to that in the other physical commodities. Seasonality matters less in the industrial metals than

Exhibit 8-4 Copper Price and Inventory Comparison, 1981–1999

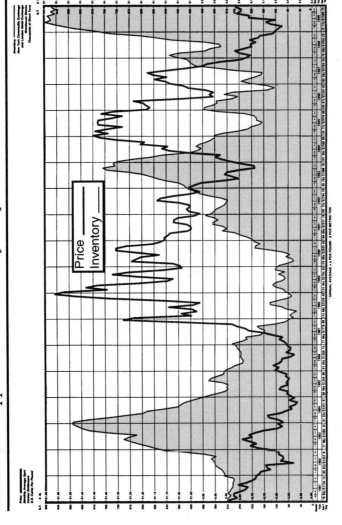

SOURCE: *The Copper Journal*, J. E. Gross & Associates, Inc.

Exhibit 8-5 1998, 1999, and 2000 Copper Spreads

	1/2/98		2/2/98		3/2/98		4/2/98		5/1/98		6/1/98	
Jan	76.20											
Feb	76.85	0.65	78.60									
Mar	77.45	0.60	78.85	0.25	78.60							
Apr	78.00	0.55	79.35	0.50	79.30	0.70	76.75					
May	78.45	0.45	79.70	0.35	79.85	0.55	77.20	0.45	84.60			
Jun	78.95	0.50	80.00	0.30	80.20	0.35	77.60	0.40	85.05	0.45	75.50	
Jul			80.35	0.35	80.50	0.30	78.05	0.45	85.40	0.35	75.95	0.45
Aug					80.90	0.40	78.40	0.35	84.80	-0.60	76.30	0.35
Sep							78.80	0.40	84.60	-0.20	76.55	0.25
Oct									84.50	-0.10	76.85	0.30
Nov											76.95	0.10
Dec												
Jan												
Feb												
Mar												
Apr												
May												

	1/4/99		2/2/99		3/2/99		4/5/99		5/3/99		6/3/99	
Jan	64.45											
Feb	64.90	0.45	64.40									
Mar	65.40	0.50	64.85	0.45	62.15							
Apr	65.85	0.45	65.35	0.50	62.55	0.40	62.50					
May	66.30	0.45	65.70	0.35	63.00	0.45	63.00	0.50	72.40			
Jun	66.75	0.45	66.00	0.30	63.45	0.45	63.40	0.40	72.80	0.40	62.10	
Jul			66.40	0.40	63.75	0.30	63.80	0.40	73.30	0.50	62.40	0.30
Aug					64.10	0.35	64.15	0.35	73.65	0.35	62.90	0.50
Sep							64.55	0.40	74.00	0.35	63.35	0.45
Oct									74.30	0.30	63.75	0.40
Nov											64.15	0.40
Dec												
Jan												
Feb												
Mar												
Apr												
May												

	1/5/00		2/4/00		3/6/00		4/6/00		5/5/00		6/5/00	
Jan	84.75											
Feb	85.20	0.45	82.35									
Mar	85.65	0.45	82.75	0.40	79.35							
Apr	86.00	0.35	83.25	0.50	79.90	0.55	76.00					
May	86.30	0.30	83.75	0.50	80.45	0.55	76.35	0.35	83.80			
Jun	86.50	0.20	84.20	0.45	80.95	0.50	76.75	0.40	83.95	0.15	79.70	
Jul			84.60	0.40	81.35	0.40	77.20	0.45	84.05	0.10	80.20	0.50
Aug					81.70	0.35	77.55	0.35	83.70	-0.35	80.40	0.20
Sep							77.90	0.35	83.70	0.00	80.65	0.25
Oct									83.80	0.10	80.75	0.10
Nov											80.85	0.10
Dec												
Jan												
Feb												
Mar												
Apr												
May												

DATA SOURCE: Bloomberg L. P.

7/1/98		8/3/98		9/1/98		10/1/98		11/2/98		12/2/98	
72.00											
72.35	0.35	74.50									
72.50	0.15	75.00	0.50	76.60							
72.80	0.30	75.20	0.20	76.35	-0.25	72.90					
73.00	0.20	75.40	0.20	76.10	-0.25	73.25	0.35	72.40			
73.30	0.30	75.70	0.30	75.90	-0.20	73.50	0.25	72.80	0.40	68.85	
		75.90	0.20	75.95	0.05	73.70	0.20	73.15	0.35	69.45	0.60
				76.15	0.20	74.00	0.30	73.40	0.25	69.85	0.40
						74.25	0.25	73.65	0.25	70.25	0.40
								73.95	0.30	70.60	0.35
										71.00	0.40

7/2/99		8/2/99		9/2/99		10/1/99		11/1/99		12/1/99	
75.75											
76.15	0.40	74.45									
76.50	0.35	74.80	0.35	79.60							
76.75	0.25	75.15	0.35	80.10	0.50	80.70					
77.00	0.25	75.50	0.35	80.60	0.50	81.10	0.40	80.15			
77.20	0.20	75.85	0.35	81.05	0.45	81.50	0.40	80.50	0.35	78.90	
		78.90	3.05	81.00	-0.05	81.80	0.30	80.95	0.45	79.75	0.85
				81.15	0.15	82.20	0.40	81.35	0.40	80.20	0.45
						82.55	0.35	81.80	0.45	80.65	0.45
								82.00	0.20	81.05	0.40
										81.45	0.40

7/5/00		8/4/00		9/5/00		10/5/00	
81.35							
81.80	0.45	87.05					
82.25	0.45	87.30	0.25	90.60			
82.25	0.00	87.40	0.10	90.90	0.30	90.95	
82.30	0.05	87.60	0.20	91.05	0.15	90.90	-0.05
82.40	0.10	87.80	0.20	91.25	0.20	91.10	0.20
		87.60	-0.20	91.30	0.05	90.75	-0.35
				91.35	0.05	90.65	-0.10
						90.60	-0.05

in the grain and energy markets. True, manufacturing has its slow
seasons, but this seems to be less of an issue than in the other markets. Yet the storage imperatives play an important role, the more so
because here they tell you about manufacturing activity—demand.

The spreads for 1998 and 1999, shown in Exhibit 8-5, reflect some
of the story of Exhibit 8-6, which shows the price-stocks relationship from 1995 through the first half of 2000.

These futures price readings, taken close to the first of the month
as they are, show strongly positive spreads during the first quarter
of 1998. Stocks reached a peak relative to the previous 3 years, a
sign that the storage signal at least coincided with slack demand
for copper. During April, the signal weakened until, on May 1, the
back-month spreads inverted. This signal coincides with a rather
large draw down of stocks.

The one anomaly in the spreads is the negative spreads of
September 1, 1998. However, the increasingly stronger storage signals in the spreads in the months after this find an echo in the sharp
buildup of warehouse inventories during these months.

The 1999 spreads give fairly strong storage signals during most
of that year. They weaken slightly in June and August. This probably means no more than slight inventory variations during that
year. In general, demand for copper was weak, and the storage
impulse was strong. The futures prices reinforced this storage signal all through the year. Exhibit 8-6 tells the same story.

Exhibit 8-7 covers much of the same territory as Exhibit 8-6 but
brings the data forward through September 2000. You can see that
from a February inventory peak of 1 million tons, stocks fell steadily
to September's 500,000 tons. At the same time, the futures spreads for
2000, shown in Exhibit 8-5, were strongly positive through February.
After that, they weakened, although not in a straight line, until by
early October they had inverted.

During this 8-month period, prices rose, but not by any exciting
amount. Even so, the market seems to be expressing an ever-
stronger demand for copper. By early October 2000, the message
had taken on an imperative tone—don't you dare store copper.

Given how close to the source the copper tributary flows into the
manufacturing mainstream, this should alert you to look for further
signs of activity in several manufacturing sectors—including all
things relating to housing, electronics, and automotive components.

Exhibit 8-6 1995–2000 Stocks and Price Chart

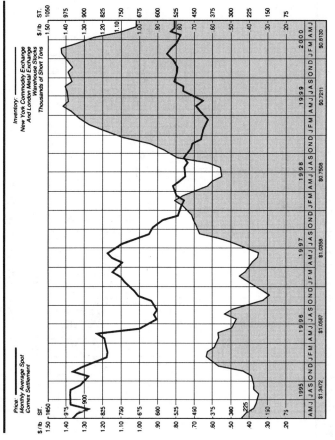

SOURCE: *The Copper Journal*, J. E. Gross & Associates, Inc.

Exhibit 8-7 Copper Stocks versus Prices

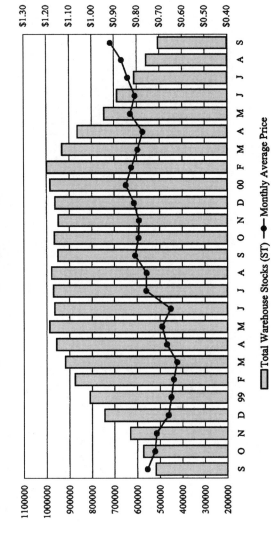

Comex & LME Warehouse Stocks Versus
Spot Comex Monthly Average Price

Spot Comex Monthly Average

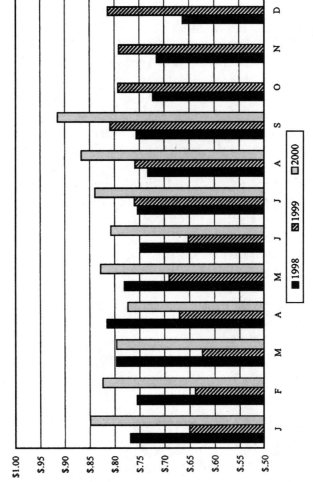

SOURCE: *The Copper Journal*, J. E. Gross & Associates, Inc.

The LME Markets Reinforce
the Copper Story

Along with copper, the LME trades futures on five other industrial metals—aluminum, lead, nickel, tin, and zinc. Only aluminum, of these five, plays as major a role in manufacturing as
steel and copper. Its uses in automotive components, household
appliances, structural members for airplanes, and construction
materials are well known. Lead-acid batteries account for 70 percent of the demand for lead. Another significant use is as x-ray
shields. The glass of television tubes and computer monitor
screens contains lead to prevent escape of the x-rays that generate
the images. Nickel, tin, and zinc have few independent uses. Yet
they figure greatly in alloys with steel, copper, or aluminum.

What matters in the context of this discussion is that all these
metals are primarily demand driven. Their roles in all areas of
manufacturing are such that an inventory draw down should be an
early warning that other signs of economic life are in the offing.
Exhibit 8-8 shows the inventory-price relationships for the remain-
ing five base metals.

Keep in mind that producers only send metal to the warehouses
when they can find nothing else to do with it. It should follow that
these diminishing stocks provide early warning that manufacturing is poised to pick up steam in the near future.

Unfortunately, LME data are less easily available than COMEX
copper data. Yet the copper and aluminum markets seem to operate nearly enough in concert that the copper market can serve as
signal enough on its own.

Oil Matters in Evaluating
the Potential for Inflation

Economic analysts attempting to measure inflation often express a
preference for a version of the Consumer Price Index (CPI) that
excludes food and energy prices, the so-called core CPI. This seems
misguided. The fact that oil prices tend not to be helpful forecasters because they are so prone to the distortions of supply shocks or
that certain commodity indexes seem less helpful because of their
overdependence on these prices should not be taken to imply that
oil prices are not significant parts of the overall inflation picture.

Exhibit 8-8 Base Metal Inventory-Price Relationships

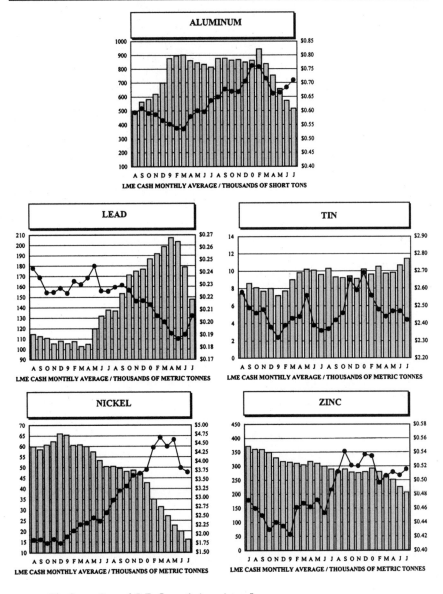

SOURCE: *The Copper Journal*, J. E. Gross & Associates, Inc.

You need go back only as far as 1999 to see why this is so. Inflation was rising. From June 1999 to February 2000, the Fed felt compelled to boost its fed funds target, in a series of six steps, from 4.75 to 6.50 percent. Most of the increase in consumer prices (read inflation) to which the Fed was reacting resulted from rising energy prices. Excluding energy, the year-over-year increase in the CPI trended lower during much of 1999. Yet the Fed moved aggressively against inflation, as well it should have.

The Fed has indicated that it tends to judge the inflationary environment by excluding the energy and food components of the various general price indexes, but the situation in 1999 raises questions about why it does. According to the Fed, the reasons for excluding energy and food prices include the tendency of these prices to exhibit a great deal of month-to-month volatility and for their behavior to be dominated by temporary supply factors rather than demand factors.

If prices are rising because of temporary supply factors, the Fed apparently believes, this will result in only short bursts of inflation, followed by a return to the prior lower trend. The Fed's thinking, apparently, is that because changes in monetary policy do not affect demand conditions significantly for several quarters, during which time the supply factors pushing up prices may have subsided, responding to supply-dominated price changes might contribute to more volatility in production and prices than it's worth.

Perhaps. One problem with the Fed logic, at least with regard to how stock prices react to oil price changes, is that the reactions tend to be asymmetric. Catherine Shalen, a Chicago Board of Trade economist, has noted that when oil prices rise, stocks that are sensitive to oil prices, such as those of transportation companies, lose value almost at once. But when oil prices revert to lower levels, the stock prices respond only slowly. Consumers know this, too. When the price of crude oil rises, prices at the gas pumps reflect the increase immediately. When crude oil prices drop, the prices consumers pay at the pump respond with a considerable lag.

But it seems doubtful that wage earners exclude food and energy price changes when they are figuring their real compensation growth. If the prices of groceries and gasoline are going up and the prices of the other things purchased are not falling commensurately, then, unless wages are rising at the same rate as the all-items

CPI, real wage growth is slowing. Most workers, other than economists, do not calculate their core real wage rate.

The year-over-year percentage change in the CPI-adjusted Employment Cost Index during late 1998 and early 1999 showed that workers' real compensation growth peaked at 2.2 percent in the third quarter of 1998 and slowed to half that, 1.1 percent, by the second quarter of 1999. It seems unlikely that workers really care whether it was the price of gasoline or the price of economists' services that slowed their real compensation growth. Workers no doubt felt poorer by the second quarter of 1999, never mind why, and in all likelihood found it at least an annoyance that a wage dollar wasn't going as far as it had just a year earlier.

This confusion about whether to look at core CPI or all-items CPI seems more important because of all the confusion about whether the U.S. economy has entered a new era and the "rules" have changed. The economic era is the same, for all that this is the twenty-first century, and inflation remains a monetary phenomenon. The advent of computers has not changed this.

A frequent claim by the "new era" people is that increased productivity growth in recent years is one factor contributing to the declining trend in inflation. Because of this declining trend in consumer inflation, labor was willing to accept slower nominal growth in compensation because its real compensation still was growing faster. Indeed, growth in the CPI-adjusted Employment Cost Index did move up in 1997 and 1998, but the trend turned downward in 1999, along with the upturn in energy prices.

When rising energy prices lead to higher consumer inflation, you can expect to see nominal compensation growth start to pick up. Following this, the prices of nonenergy goods are likely to start rising faster. When this happens, even Fed officials should be able to understand that their real wages are falling and decide to take action. Either they will negotiate an increase in their nominal wages, or they will raise interest rates to slow the nonenergy inflation. However, by waiting until core inflation responds to faster nominal wage growth, these Fed officials will have to be more aggressive in their tightening actions to accomplish their goals.

In fact, shortly after the 1999 downturn in the Employment Cost Index, the Fed did embark on a series of four tightening moves. At the November 16, 1999 FOMC meeting, the Fed boosted its fed funds target 25 basis points to 5.50 percent. Apparently, this wasn't enough to rein in inflation because the February 2, 2000 and March 21, 2000 FOMC meetings brought about two more 25-basis-point boosts to bring the target to 6.00 percent. Finally, on May 16, the FOMC decided it had to hit even harder and rammed the target up another 50 basis points to 6.50 percent.

Apparently, energy prices do matter when it comes to questions of inflation, even though their sensitivity to supply shocks renders them problematic as forecasting tools.

The Trouble with Gold

Gold used to be considered the inflation hedge par excellence. Herbert Hoover is reported to have said to FDR: "We have gold because we cannot trust governments." Investors thinking they were seeing signs of rising inflation would shift assets into gold for protection. A rising gold price, then, signaled that at least some people were anticipating dangerous economic times ahead.

This view of gold as inflation hedge is not hard to understand. In 1989, George Gero, a New York gold trader, explained the attraction of gold for this use by noting that during the Great Depression of the 1930s, a kilo of gold (35.36 troy ounces) would have bought a new Chevrolet, Ford, or Plymouth. A kilo of gold would still have bought a new Chevrolet, Ford, or Plymouth in 1989.

Gero also mentioned that the 1989 car buyer might well have used the same physical kilo as the 1930s car buyer. Virtually all the gold ever mined still exists. Yet it would be a mistake to equate the physical permanence of gold with permanent value. The 1999 kilo will no longer buy a new car, not even a small Ford or Chevrolet. Chrysler has quit making Plymouths, of course, but the kilo won't quite buy even the smallest Dodge.

In *The Power of Gold*, Peter L. Bernstein makes the same point even more graphically with reference to the Dow Jones Industrial Average:

> By some remarkable coincidence, the Dow Jones Industrial Average of stock prices was at just about 850 when gold touched its 850 peak [actually, the Dow closed January 1980 at 860.34]. Thus, an ounce of gold would have bought one share of the Average at that moment. When gold was down to the

$300 area in the summer of 1999, however, the Dow Jones was around 10,000. Now more than thirty ounces of gold would be needed to buy one share of the Average [p. 361].

It has been pointed out that by the early 1980s, investors had many ways available to them to protect their investments from the ravages of inflation. That era saw double-digit bond yields, and the stock market was gaining at a rate that more than made up for inflation. Gold, as Bernstein notes, pays no dividend or interest income, and it is expensive to store.

Worse, during the decades of the 1980s and 1990s, the U.S. price of gold came to be more nearly a function of Fed policy than anything else. As Bernstein says, "Holding gold can make little sense if inflation is dead or dying, because then there is little hope of recouping the storage costs and offsetting the lost income."

During this period, too, gold could be seen to suffer some of the same kinds of supply problems that often make it hard to rely on signals from the oil and grain markets. Two of the biggest sources of new gold were South Africa and Russia, and those supplies were subject to a variety of political factors.

Even before the breakup of the Soviet Union, the Russians felt compelled to sell large amounts of gold to raise the currency to buy the goods needed to make up for failed crops and a disappointing factory system. Other countries used their gold reserves in similar ways. These activities further cloud any signal gold might give about rising inflation.

Bernstein begins the prologue to his fascinating book by citing a chilling story told by the English Victorian writer John Ruskin about "a man who boarded a ship carrying his entire wealth in a large bag of gold coins. A terrible storm came up a few days into the voyage and the alarm went off to abandon ship. Strapping the bag around his waist, the man went up on deck, jumped overboard, and promptly sank to the bottom of the sea. Asks Ruskin: 'Now, as he was sinking, had he the gold? Or had the gold him?'" (p. 1).

Bernstein comes back to this story because it surely seems that when people—be they legendary characters like King Midas or more recent and very real leaders like Charles de Gaulle—put too much faith in gold, the gold invariably ends up having them.

9

Changing Rules and Noisy Markets

As if trying to figure out what the markets will do weren't hard enough in the best of times, every so often an indicator that has seemed reliable for a long time mysteriously quits working. Eventually, you can figure out why, but, until you do, such an indicator failure can be maddening.

Three kinds of situations can mess up the signals of any of these indicators. Somebody can change the rules in the middle of the game—rather as if a baseball umpire would change the strike zone in the middle of an inning. Something like this seems to have happened to the U.S. Treasury yield curve. The markets can change. The success of Eurodollar futures seems to have been the major factor causing the demise of Treasury-bill futures. At times, the markets can just get noisy. It is rather like a radio station not quite coming in. You can almost hear the broadcast, but major static makes it difficult to know exactly what's being said. This happened in 1999 because of the Y2K furor.

Rules changes and market shifts are the more troubling because they tend to be permanent, or at least long-term, changes. These are what market insiders often refer to as *secular changes*. The structure of the market has become different from what it was before. Noisy markets fall in the category of *temporary changes*, even though the phenomenon causing the noise can endure, in some cases, for many months. They create extra work, but you can often filter out the noise and figure out what you need to know.

Deregulating a Good Indicator

During the 1980s and very early 1990s, the fed funds versus 10-year Treasury-note spread proved an especially useful indicator. This spread embodied the classic Wicksellian base rate versus the natural rate idea, with the fed funds rate as the base and the 10-year Treasury note serving as a useful proxy for the unobservable natural interest rate.

The idea is that if the fed funds rate were holding steady but 10-year Treasury-note yields were rising, the resulting widening of the spread between them signaled an expansionary posture on the part of the Federal Reserve (Fed). Then economic activity could be expected to pick up—with a lag. Keep in mind that it was the relationship, not the absolute yield level, that gave forecasters a place to hang their hats with regard to the Fed's monetary policy. In fact, during the 35 years from 1955 through 1990, changes in this spread tended to lead U.S. industrial production growth by about two quarters.

Interestingly, a forecaster using this spread during the late 1980s would have seemed far better tuned into the economic pulse than most of his or her colleagues. Just after the stock market crash of 1987, most forecasters predicted sluggish U.S. economic growth at best. Some even predicted a recession. Contrary to what the forecasters were saying, this market indicator signaled an economic pickup and the subsequent need for the Fed to tighten policy.

In the fourth quarter of 1987, the fed funds–10-year Treasury-note spread was 199 basis points. In the first quarter of 1988, it was 155 basis points. Historically, spreads this wide signaled a very easy monetary policy and that the Fed was trying to promote growth. As it turned out, economic activity was quite robust in 1988, as evidenced by the 5 percent growth in industrial production that occurred that year.

Then, in the spring of 1989, the rate spread was very narrow: −100 basis points. In the past, a spread this negative suggested a restrictive policy. Again, the consensus among forecasters conflicted with the auction-market signals. Where many economists thought there would be higher interest rates and a strong economy, prices dived, and the negative yield spread suggested the need for easing—which the Fed did. The result was slow growth for the rest of the year.

Yet, from late 1990 to the present, the fed funds–10-year Treasury-note spread has ceased to generate reliable signals. Looking back, it seems to have been one of those cases where the umpires changed the rules in the middle of the game.

The Effect of Deposit-Rate Deregulation on the Relationship between the Yield Curve and Economic Growth

The relationship between the long-short yield spread and the pace of economic activity has been changed by the deregulation of deposit-rate ceilings. In 1984, federally imposed ceilings on deposit interest rates were abolished for all deposit classes except for demand deposits. This had the effect of diminishing the interest sensitivity of the demand for bank and thrift deposits. Prior to deregulation, a rise in open-market interest rates above regulated deposit ceiling interest rates would induce households and corporations to lower their demand for deposits and increase their demand for nondeposit fixed-income investments. In and of itself, this shift in demand did *not* lower the amount of deposits in the economy but rather changed the composition of those deposits away from savings and time deposits toward transactions deposits. The fall in the demand for deposits brought on by the rise in open-market interest rates above deposit ceiling rates implied that a given amount of deposits would now "support," or be consistent with, a higher dollar amount of transactions. Economists refer to this as an *increase in the velocity of money*. Conversely, when open-market interest rates fell below deposit rates, households and corporations would increase their demand for deposits. This meant that a given level of deposits would now support a lower dollar amount of transactions. That is, the velocity of money would have fallen.

Typically, a steepening in the yield curve—that is, the yield on longer-maturity fixed-income securities rising relative to the yield on shorter-maturity ones—has been associated with increased growth in bank and thrift deposits. All else the same, an increase in the growth of bank deposits would imply an increase in the growth of the economy. If a steepening yield curve also resulted in open-market interest rates rising above deposit ceiling rates, then the velocity of money would have been expected to increase. Therefore, in the era in which there were federally imposed ceilings on deposit rates, a steeper yield curve would have been associated not only with faster growth in bank and thrift deposits but also with an increase in the velocity of the increased supply of deposits. Thus there would be two effects working in tandem to increase economic growth.

Following elimination of deposit-rate ceilings in 1984, the interest-rate sensitivity of the demand for deposits diminished. As open-market interest rates rose, banks and thrifts were now allowed to raise their deposit offering rates in a competitive manner. Thus there was less of an interest-rate incentive for the public to lower its demand for deposits. As a result, the velocity of deposits would not rise as much as open-market rates rose, and the yield curve steepened. So, a steepening yield curve might still be associated with faster deposit growth but not an increase in velocity. After deposit-rate deregulation, then, a given spread between the yield on longer-maturity fixed-income securities and shorter-maturity ones would imply future economic growth slower than was the case before the deregulation.

The Treasury Buyback
Distorts a Useful Indicator

The common wisdom, for years, has been that the shape of the U.S. Treasury yield curve provides a good indication of whether the U.S. economy is heading toward recession or a period of growth. The thinking has been that an inverted yield curve—one showing long-term yields going below short-term yields—signals the approach of a recession, or at least a period that will see markedly slower growth.

Yet, when the U.S. Treasury yield curve inverted in the late winter of 2000, economic growth didn't show any signs of slowing. The strength of the economic numbers was such that the Fed felt compelled to boost its fed funds target another 75 basis points in two moves in March and May. Also, as you have seen in the earlier discussion of yield curves, the Treasury yield curve and the AAA yield curve, which have stayed close to parallel in recent history, parted company. When the Treasury yield curve inverted, the AAA yield curve did not. In this case, the AAA yield curve more nearly reflected the actual situation than did the Treasury yield curve.

The reasons for the separation of the two yield curves and the failure of the U.S. Treasury yield curve signal are not hard to find. For some time, the Treasury has been cutting back on its issuance of longer-term debt and reducing the frequency of the auctions. Where the Treasury used to hold four 30-year bond auctions a year and issue about $11 billion each time, it now holds two auctions and issues about $8 billion at a time. As if this weren't enough, the Treasury embarked on a well-publicized program to buy back large amounts of outstanding debt.

Because of these changes in Treasury policy with regard to longer-term debt issuance, auction frequency, and the buyback program, the inversion of the Treasury yield curve in early 2000 seems more a symptom of a severe supply shortage than a sign of a shift in market demand for credit. As a result, it issued a misleading signal in February and March 2000. Ultimately, the market may adapt to this new situation, and the yield curve may again prove helpful. For the foreseeable future, though, the AAA yield curve seems to promise more reliable results.

The Traditional TED Was Not "Too Big to Fail"

Two changes in U.S. Treasury policy seem to have caused the Treasury yield curve to send out misleading signals. Something similar happened to the traditional Treasury-bill futures–Eurodollar futures (TED) spread. When the government decided Continental Illinois Bank was too big to fail, the TED ceased to be a reliable indicator.

The traditional TED was additionally harmed by the drying up of the Treasury-bill (T-bill) futures market. Huge as the underlying T-bill market is, T-bill futures simply don't matter anymore. The most likely explanation seems to be that T-bill futures are victims of the success of Eurodollar futures. The volume and open-interest statistics certainly tell an interesting story.

Open interest is a measure of the number of contracts outstanding. For every futures buyer, there must be a seller. Further, to remove a position from the books, the buyer must sell, and the seller must buy. For example, when one trader buys one Eurodollar (ED) contract from a second trader, this creates two contracts of volume and establishes two open (unresolved positions)—that is, an open interest of two. Then, if the first trader, having bought from the second trader, now sells his or her contract to a third trader, this resolves one of the open positions. The second trader's position remains open, so far. Futures market users watch open interest because it provides a measure of the depth and liquidity of the market.

The futures markets have never seen open interest to equal that of the Eurodollar market. On an October 2000 day, the *Wall Street Journal* showed the following volume and open-interest data for T-bill and ED futures:

	Volume	Open interest
T-bills	14	1,340
Eurodollars	322,601	3,051,347

Both contracts have a par value of $1 million. This means that by multiplying Eurodollar open interest by $1 million, you can see that the notional principal outstanding has a par value of 3.05^{12}, or $3 trillion and change. The T-bill notional principal outstanding is $1.34 billion.

Interest-rate futures thrive largely because they have risk-management utility. Portfolio managers use Eurodollars to create synthetic swaps and to hedge swap positions. They use Treasury note and bond futures to create synthetic exposures to bond indexes, to adjust the interest-rate sensitivity of fixed-income portfolios, and to adjust asset allocations on a temporary, tactical basis.

When the London InterBank Offered Rate (LIBOR) became the floating-rate benchmark for the swap market and interest-rate swaps became the risk-management tool of choice for the corporate treasuries of the world, T-bills simply lost relevance, while LIBOR-based Eurodollars gained—all out of proportion to what T-bills lost. End of indicator.

Markets Can Get Noisy

Rule changes and changes in the marketplace are bad enough. In addition to these factors, markets sometimes get noisy. Even though prices are bouncing around and spreads are widening or narrowing in tantalizing ways, it may not mean anything. Year-end is a tricky time because portfolio managers are doing their year-end book cleanup. At times, journalists get hold of a story they can't seem to let go of, and their reports can make it difficult to see what is really going on. In some cases, the complex nature of the markets or a market event that has escaped notice obscures vision.

Year-End Window Dressing

The approach of year-end creates interesting accounting and regulatory challenges for banks, insurance companies, mutual funds, and pension funds. As portfolio managers scurry around to pretty up the window displays, their activity can distort certain market signals.

A bank, for example, with a capital-to-assets ratio pushing the upper limits of what regulations allow, might want to shorten its balance sheet temporarily for reasons having to do with the regulations governing capital adequacy. In this case, it wouldn't bid as aggressively on new assets. Also, because it doesn't want to have to show any borrowing from the Fed, it might sit on reserves it would otherwise lend out in the fed funds market as a precautionary measure. Other banks, short on reserves, must then bid up the cost of this credit to a level that will pry the funds they need loose. Enough of this happens to impart an upward bias to the fed funds and Eurodollar markets during December and January.

A similar distortion can result from mutual fund activity. A large number of mutual funds end their fiscal years on October 31. While conclusive data on this are elusive, close observers of the mutual fund market seem convinced that they see significant amounts of tax-loss selling during the month of October. This seems to account for a fair fraction of the downward pressure on stocks in October 1999 and 2000. Along with this, people often seem to wait until after the first of the year to put new money into mutual funds. As a result, the funds typically experience large inflows of cash in the first week of January. Again, this can distort the market signal briefly.

The Y2K Furor

You no doubt recall that as the year 2000 approached, so did a potentially large computer programming concern. Older software used a date format that included only the last two digits of the year—99 rather than 1999. This wasn't a problem in terms of computers recognizing dates as long as the first two digits were assumed to be 19. But it wasn't obvious that the computer systems of corporations, financial institutions, and governmental units would be able to cope with the switch to the new century.

Fortunately, the massive effort employed to make everybody "Y2K compliant" seems to have paid off, and this little story has a happy ending. Still, the attending furor about the potential for problems did create market noise.

For one thing, the markets feared that there could be a major liquidity crisis. That is, a large-scale computer system malfunction could close off access to banks and other sources of funds needed for ongoing operations. Because of this fear, many firms sat on cash that otherwise would have been deposited or invested. This caused the money base to balloon toward the end of 1999, as Exhibit 9-1 shows.

You can see how the money baseline on the chart seems to follow a smooth upward slope except for the short period right around the turn of the year. The 3-month TED peaked earlier, of course, because it involves securities that would have matured, and so supplied cash, 3 months forward. These developments warned investors and analysts of the need for extra caution when looking at any of the market indicators.

Markets Bundle Risks

Credit spreads can be useful because these spreads between corporate and U.S. Treasury yields tend to widen markedly in advance of recessions or periods of sharply slower growth. In a study published by the Federal Reserve Bank of Chicago in 1992, James H. Stock and Mark W. Watson took a fresh look at leading, coincident, and lagging indicators with an eye to revising the lists being used by forecasters. In their new list of leading indicators, they included a credit spread, but their model had problems.

More recently, in a study published by the Federal Reserve Bank of Dallas, John V. Duca took another look at credit spreads and

Exhibit 9-1 Interest-Rate Spread (3-Month LIBOR less 3-Month T-Bill) versus Adjusted Monetary Base

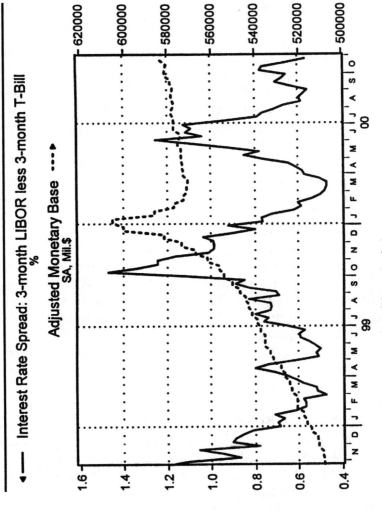

SOURCE: Bureau of Economic Analysis/Haver Analytics

concluded that while they continue to be rich sources of information, they must be interpreted with caution because, in many cases, they bundle three kinds of risk: prepayment risk, liquidity risk, and default (credit) risk. The first two can create noise that can obscure the signal of the last one.

The idea that the spread between corporate and U.S. Treasury yields is a complex bundle of risks shouldn't surprise anyone. For some time it has been fashionable to see all financial securities as bundles of this kind. A mortgage security, for example, is obviously a bond plus an embedded call option (the homeowners' prepayment rights behave like a call feature in a corporate bond). Callable and putable corporate bonds can be analyzed as bundles of a bond and one or more options.

Even relatively simple-seeming securities such as U.S. Treasury securities or stocks lend themselves to such analyses. A stock can be seen to be a bundle of call options on the company's future earnings. A Treasury yield contains at least two components: the real interest rate and an inflation premium. The yield of a corporate bond contains these two components plus the credit spread, which itself might have as many as three components, following Duca.

Prepayment risk arises from the fact that, as with a mortgage or callable corporate bond, should the issuer call the bond away, the bondholder can suffer loss. Because of this loss potential, investors demand a yield premium for taking the risk.

Liquidity risk arises from the fact that, once issued, many corporate bonds never trade again and more trade only intermittently. This illiquidity exposes investors to the risk that they may not be able to get out of a position when they want to, at least not at a viable price. Facing this possibility, they again demand a yield premium.

Default risk is credit risk—the chance that the issuer will not meet its obligations to pay interest on time. The premium investors charge for taking this risk is the true credit spread, but you can see that the other two risks can blur the picture.

Duca mentions that "at first glance, the widening of the spread between yields on 10-year Baa-rated corporate and Treasury bonds in late 1998 might suggest the risk of impending recession. However, a less alarming picture emerges from decomposing this spread into the yield spread between Aaa- and Baa-rated bonds and the yield spread between the highest grade corporate bond (Aaa) and Treasuries." (Note that Duca is using Moody's credit rating designations, where Aaa is equivalent to S&P AAA and Baa is equivalent to S&P BBB.)

The Aaa-Baa component, Duca goes on to say, rose far less in 1998 than the Aaa-Treasury component, and it is the former component that more nearly reflects the default risk that correlates well with economic downturns. Prepayment and liquidity premium changes show little correlation with recessions.

This seems a good point, but there is an easier way to filter out the prepayment and liquidity noise. The Fannie Mae and Freddie Mac issues that underlie agency futures are hugely liquid and noncallable. As a result, the U.S. Treasury–agency (TAG) spreads (discussed in Chapter 5) would seem to clear up this issue. This may be as close to a pure credit spread as you can get.

Fake Flights to Quality

The term *flight to quality* was much bandied about throughout the year 2000. Few, if any, of the market events cited seem to have been true flights to quality, so these claims seem like another kind of market noise that careful investors should be at pains to filter out. Flights to quality typically occur, if they do at all, when events external to the market threaten its stability.

During the last days of the Soviet Union, for example, an attempted "palace coup" against Gorbachev touched off such a flight. At that time, the West German economy seemed much the strongest and most promising to international investors. Consequently, investment funds had been pouring into German government bonds and into the stocks of German companies for some time. But suddenly this troubling situation loomed in Russia, not all that far from the German border. When something like this happens, investors want their money in the safest securities in the most politically stable country they can find. Most often, this means they flee to U.S. Treasury securities. The U.S. Treasury market was a huge benefactor as investors sought safe haven from stormy Europe.

Domestically, when market analysts see investors fleeing the stock market and putting money in U.S. Treasury securities, they often refer to it as a flight to quality. A stock price can go to zero, after all, but U.S. Treasury securities are free of default risk. These investments may not earn exciting yields, but at least the principal will be safe. This makes them higher quality than almost anything else.

Something like this happened in late January 1994. The denizens of the futures floors at the Chicago Mercantile Exchange and the Chicago Board of Trade were buzzing about huge trades in Standard and Poor's (S&P) 500 futures and U.S. Treasury note futures. By way of background, street talk at the time was that with threatening signs of inflation popping up all around, the Fed was going to have to raise its fed funds target, maybe by quite a lot. (At the beginning of 1994, recall, the fed funds target was 3 percent. By February 1995, the Fed had driven the target all the way to 6 percent.) This would slow economic growth enough to tame inflation, but it could also kick the pins out from under the stock market.

Responding to these concerns, one of the major broker-dealers acted for a pension fund client, according to market chatter, to sell tens of thousands of contracts of S&P 500 futures and to buy tens of thousands of Treasury note futures contracts. This pair of futures market moves reduced the pension fund's exposure to a potentially adverse move in the stock market and, in effect, parked the money in safer U.S. Treasury securities. If its concerns about what higher interest rates could mean bore out, the pension fund could later substitute actual stock sales and Treasury note purchases for the futures. If the concerns evaporated, the futures would be easily reversed. The point is that this was a classic flight-to-quality move in anticipation of trouble in the market.

Several situations arose during 2000 that stirred up talk about flight-to-quality phenomena—inflation fears early in the year were followed by a mid-April stock market plunge and then by the summer oil crisis and the October problems in the Middle East. All these events caused talk about flight to quality, most of which seems misguided.

The April 14, 2000 stock market collapse intrigued Howard Simons as much for what didn't happen as for what did. Commenting on that event in TheStreet.com, he said, "What did not happen was a flight to quality bond market rally." He goes on to claim that of the 17 daily declines of 3.5 percent or more in the S&P 500 since the 1987 crash, only 1987 saw a genuine flight to quality and concludes that flights to quality are more an urban legend than a real market phenomenon.

Perhaps. At the very least, when assessing the possibility of such an event occurring, you should ask whether the market really has anything to be afraid of. The U.S. stock market sold off Monday, January 24, 2000. Again, flight-to-quality talk surfaced in the discussions of what might be going on. At that time, stock market analyst Helene Meisler commented, "We see flights to quality when there's a reason to be scared." After saying she'd found nothing in the recent news to motivate sufficient fear for a flight, she concluded, "Once again, it's the press searching for a reason that just doesn't fit the logic."

Further Press-Induced Noise

Financial journalists can sometimes create a great deal of noise. Something like this happened in the summer and fall of 1997. With the tenth anniversary of the 1987 stock market crash approaching, large numbers of journalists took a notion that the parallels between the two years were striking and investors had better get ready for a repeat of the 1987 disaster.

Exhibits 9-2 and 9-3 show the superficial similarities between the 1987 and 1997 stock markets. Both topped out in August at levels well above anything ever seen before and then bobbled around before plunging sharply in October.

A deeper look suggests that the two situations weren't at all parallel. The 508-point drop in the Dow Jones Industrial Average (DJIA) in 1987 amounted to a 22.6 percent loss. The 1997 drop was bigger, 554 points, but only amounted to a 7 percent loss. The stories tended to overlook that, in the aftermath of 1987, U.S. stock exchanges built in some safety features that would have made it much harder to have the kind of freefall the markets experienced in 1987.

Finally, the 1997 market was driven, at least in significant part, by the Asian financial meltdown. There were good, knowable reasons for what was happening that year. The reasons for the 1987 crisis were elusive then and remain so now. Theories have been advanced. None seems especially satisfying.

When the press gets hold of something like this and won't let it go for a period of weeks or months, it gets harder and harder to winnow the true information from the chaff.

Exhibit 9-2 1987 Stock Market

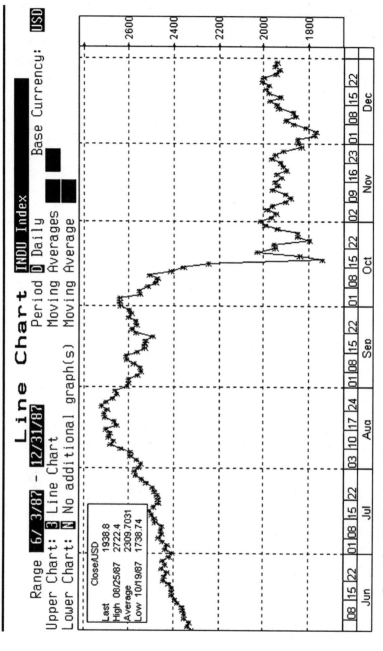

SOURCE: Copyright 2001 Bloomberg L.P.

Exhibit 9-3 1997 Stock Market

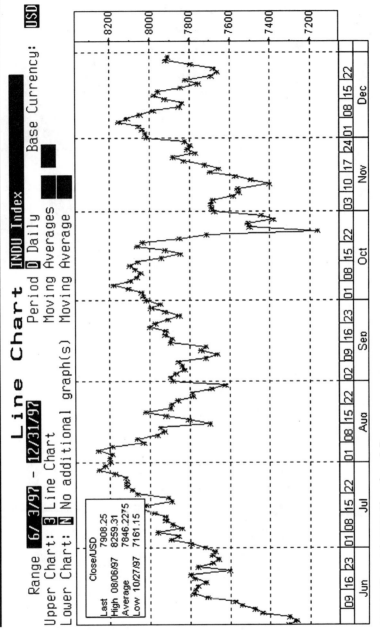

SOURCE: Copyright 2001 Bloomberg L.P.

10

Putting the Market Indicators to Work

The step from reading the market indicators to making an investment decision is neither short nor obvious. If it were, more investors would have better records. It's difficult to make money consistently in these markets. You can see just how difficult if you examine the performance reports of mutual funds. Only a small number of these professional investors consistently do better than the common market benchmarks such as the Standard and Poor's (S&P) 500 Index. Yet difficult doesn't mean impossible.

Serious investing requires a plan. Given any plan you may have settled on, the market indicators provide a framework that allows you to make sense of what is going on in the economy. Most important, the indicators can help you anticipate the market and put your investment strategies in place earlier than might otherwise be the case. This is crucial because the only way to benefit from a market move is to have invested before the events driving the move "make the news."

A Framework for Predicting and Interpreting Economic Events

The market situation of March and April 2000 provides a helpful illustration of how the market indicators give you a framework for making sense of what you see in the economy and how they can even help you anticipate developments in the market. It should be obvious how this can help shape your investment decision making.

In early spring of 2000, there wasn't an economic cloud in the sky. The Federal Reserve (Fed) was in a tightening mode, having boosted its fed funds target rate 25 basis points at its February meeting and another 25 basis points at its March meeting. Most of the financial commentators were saying that it looked like even the Fed could do nothing to slow this rampaging economy.

Yet the market indicators suggested that a slowdown was in the offing. The key indicator in this system is the width of the AAA corporate bond less fed funds yield spread. During the 6 months leading up to April 2000, this spread had narrowed considerably. As backups to this signal, commodity prices were weakening, and the spread between AAA and BBB corporate bonds was widening.

All this has implications for corporate profit growth. The rising fed funds target signaled a reluctance on the part of the Fed to create more credit. The Fed moves of early 2000 indicated that the Fed would still create credit, but for a stiffer and stiffer price. The narrowing yield spread indicated a lack of demand for credit on the part of corporate borrowers, which in turn signaled a lack of plans to buy new equipment or expand existing facilities.

Weakening industrial commodity prices further betokened a slowing of future manufacturing activity. And widening credit spreads told of the reluctance of institutional investors to buy the bonds of the corporate issuers, which is another way of saying they were reluctant to loan money to the corporations seeking to borrow.

The only way stock prices can rise is for earnings to rise relative to interest rates. This can happen in any of several ways. If interest rates are rising, earnings must rise more. If earnings are stable or sagging a bit, interest rates must be falling, and falling faster than earnings. However it happens, the gap between earnings and interest rates must widen for stock prices to increase.

Yet, despite the ebullience of the market commentators, the market indicators in March and April 2000 argued against an increase in stock prices. Interest rates were on the rise, and all the signs suggested that corporations faced stiff challenges to earnings. That is, a study of the market indicators at that time would have told you that the economy would soon slow and that the stock market was in for some bumps. You could have begun to adjust your portfolio accordingly.

This kind of hypothesis building that the market indicators help you do can make for lonely times. You will not be espousing a popular view, although this may not be all bad. After all, once this view becomes the consensus, you can no longer make money on it.

The market indicators framework can help in another way. As you watch events unfold, suppose that a rather discouraging economic number comes out. Housing starts may be down. Unit labor costs could have risen. Machine tool sales could have slowed. Those who can't imagine how anything can slow this economy would be likely to call reports such as these an aberration and assign no significance to them. For you, in contrast, this will have great interest, for it will help confirm your hypothesis that the economy will slow. This will make you more confident about your original interpretation of the market indicators.

As you know, by July 2000, you could see weakness emerging in the manufacturing sectors and hear the commentators changing their tunes. By the beginning of 2001, the market commentaries had completely lost their rosy glow. Further, the Fed felt compelled to lower its fed funds target rate. The fact that it did so in the form of a 50-basis-point move outside a scheduled meeting and then lowered the target another 50 basis points at the January 31, 2001 meeting suggests that the Fed thought strong action was required to stimulate the economy.

Curiously, in January 2001, among all the talk of doom and gloom in the financial media, the market indicators were, again, telling a different story. The yield spread was widening, and industrial metals prices were on an upswing. The metals prices signal may have needed to be approached with caution. If this were to prove to be related to supply rather than being demand-driven, it could turn out to be a false signal.

Yet consider briefly what a widening yield spread means. The Fed had lowered its fed funds target rate a total of 100 basis points (one full percentage point) in its two January 2001 moves. This meant that the Fed was willing to supply credit at a rate below what the private sector was offering. It follows that you should have seen an increase in corporate borrowing and spending going forward. Whenever such a constellation of events occurs, the economy should perk up considerably.

The one fly in the ointment was that the upsurge in metals prices could well have been related to energy prices. Recall that high energy prices caused several metals companies to curtail production or even to shut down certain plants.

Nevertheless, the market indicators were providing an all-important early warning to again be ready to shift your investment approach.

Investing a Step at a Time

On first seeing these signs of an impending economic slowdown, or of an impending upturn, you might have begun getting ready to at least scale into your investment strategy. Each subsequent confirmation of your hypothesis should prompt further action. You may, in anticipation of a slowdown, decide to hold off on buying more stock and put new capital in cash. At some point, as your confidence in your outlook grows, you may even liquidate some of your stock holdings. Farther along in the process you may begin to shift the cash you have been accumulating into bonds. As more and more signals fall into place, you can take more and more decisive investment action—within the scope of your own guidelines and plan.

Note that the assumptions here are that you will scale into and out of the various sectors and that it is extremely unlikely that you will ever be completely out of stocks or bonds. For example, using large increments to illustrate, you may begin a sequence like this with 60 percent of your capital in stocks, 30 percent in bonds, and 10 percent in cash. As you gain confidence in what the market indicators are telling you, you may shift from that 60-30-10 to 55-30-15 and ultimately to something like 50-45-5. These are not recommendations of what an asset allocation should be but made-up numbers to illustrate a shift of investment emphasis rather than a total restructuring of a portfolio.

With this as general background, you can revisit the key indicators and consider how they can help you shape your investment thinking and how they can guide your implementation of your investment plan.

The Yield Spread Provides Early Warning

The key factors in this system of market indicators are credit supply and demand. Changes in fed funds futures spreads can help you anticipate policy shifts with regard to how much credit the Fed is willing to create. Changes in the spread between the AAA corporate yield and fed funds provide a useful gauge of credit demand.

A key fact about the yield spread as a market indicator is that it consistently leads economic performance by enough to make it an extremely useful early warning for investors, as Exhibit 10-1 shows.

Here, the dotted line tracks year-over-year percentage changes in the index of coincident indicators, which is a good proxy for overall economic activity. Notice that this flattens, or drops, dramatically going into recessions, which are indicated by the shaded bars.

The yield-curve plot here makes use of a 12-month moving average, which smooths the data. Smoothing in this way means that the indicator will give fewer false signals. It also means that you will not always be the first one on the bandwagon when the market is getting ready to change, but you will have a smoother investment ride once you are on.

Crucially, the yield-curve plot describes a path similar to that of the coincident indicators but does so earlier. You can see that it gives you good lead time with its signals in every case but one, the false signal of 1990. (See Chapter 9 for a discussion of a possible reason for this misfire.)

Brokerage literature often includes a disclaimer to the effect that past performance is no guarantee of future results. The same should be said of any indicators. Indeed, there are no sure things in investing. Some of Warren Buffett's most humorous moments come when he is explaining to Baxter Hathaway shareholders what went wrong with one of his investment decisions. The best you can do is try to make the highest-probability moves possible. Clearly, the yield curve is a high-probability indicator.

In recent times, the yield curve was telling the right story at the end of 2000, even though few commentators or investors seemed to want to pay attention, as Exhibit 10-2 shows.

You can see that the yield spread began to narrow, turned down, as early as April 2000, yet the choppy path of the index of coincident indicators (here, the solid line) struggled against this signal until it finally made a decisive move downward in September. Recall, too, that the financial press was full of talk during much of this time about how robust the U.S. economy was and how little or nothing could slow it. Importantly, the yield spread was telling a different story.

Exhibit 10-1 Yield Spread (Moody's Aaa Corporate less Fed Funds) versus Composite Index of Coincident Indicators

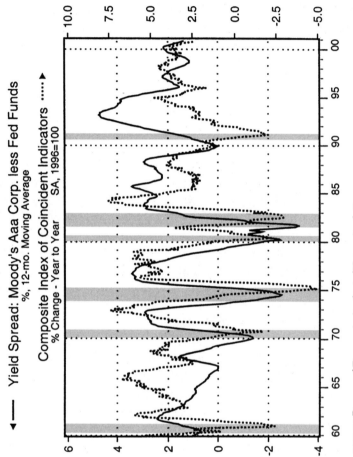

— Yield Spread: Moody's Aaa Corp. less Fed Funds
%, 12-mo. Moving Average

Composite Index of Coincident Indicators ·····▶
% Change - Year to Year   SA, 1996=100

SOURCE: Bureau of Economic Analysis/Haver Analytics

Exhibit 10-2 Composite Index of Coincident Indicators versus Yield Spread (Moody's Aaa Corporate less Fed Funds)

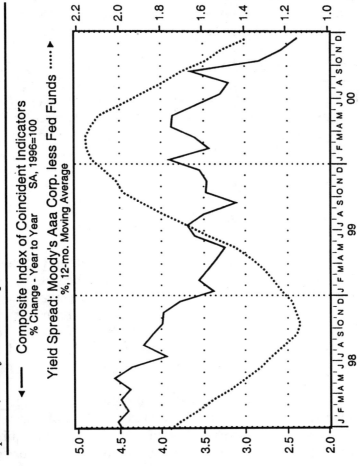

SOURCE: Bureau of Economic Analysis/Haver Analytics

Reading the Exhibits

The exhibits in this chapter present yield-curve information in a different format than the earlier chapters did. The usual yield-curve display shows yields across a range of maturities at one moment. This makes tracking yield-curve history difficult. This format tracks one curve segment in terms of the difference, or spread, between the 10-year Aaa corporate bond yield and fed funds, which makes it easy to track the history of this crucial yield-curve segment.

When the line moves up, as it does from 1990 through 1993 in Exhibit 10-1, for example, the yield spread is widening. Equivalently, the yield curve is steepening. Conversely, when the line moves down, as it does most of the time after 1993, again in Exhibit 10-1, the spread is narrowing, which is another way of saying the yield curve is flattening. Any time the line breaks below the zero line, the yield curve has inverted.

Motivating the Use of Aaa Corporate Yields

Traditionally, of course, the basis for any discussion of the yield curve as an indicator of economic health has been the Treasury yield curve. However, a number of factors have created noise in the Treasury yield signal since 1990. Prior to that time, as Exhibit 10-3 shows, the 10-year Treasury-note yield less fed funds (called *interest-rate spread*) and the Aaa corporate yield less fed funds tracked each other closely. By the early 1990s, they were tracking less well.

What this exhibit shows is that when both indicators were reacting only to economic factors and not to technical supply factors such as changes in U.S. Treasury policy, the two curves gave equivalent signals. The corporate market has not suffered the effects of deposit bailouts or Treasury buyback plans. These two factors argue, first, for the reliability of the corporate–fed funds indicator and, second, for the replacement of the Treasury–fed funds indicator with the other.

Exhibit 10-3 Interest Rate Spread (10-Year Bond less Fed Funds Rate) versus Yield Spread (Moody's Aaa Corporate less Fed Funds)

——— Interest Rate Spread: 10-Year Bond less Fed Funds Rate
%, 12-mo. Moving Average

▼ Yield Spread: Moody's Aaa Corp. less Fed Funds ·····▶
%, 12-mo. Moving Average

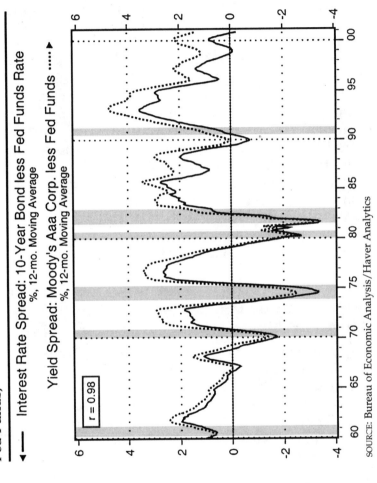

SOURCE: Bureau of Economic Analysis/Haver Analytics

Industrial Commodity Prices Should Follow the Yield Curve

Once the yield spread has changed direction, the search is on for corroboration of its signal. The next sign to look for is a shift in the price trend for industrial commodities. Exhibit 10-4 shows how the metals component of the Journal of Commerce–Economic Cycle Research Institute (JOC-ECRI) Industrial Price Index reacted after the yield spread shifts in both 1998 and 1999. Earlier, when the yield spread began widening, metals prices began climbing. More recently, after the yield spread began narrowing, metals prices began a downward trend.

The longer history presented in Exhibit 10-5 shows a similar pattern, although the match is far from perfect.

Despite the rough correspondence, the metals prices do follow changes in the yield spread with enough regularity that when you see the commodity price evidence, it should increase your confidence in your hypothesis about what the yield spread has been telling you about the condition of the economy.

Credit Spreads Provide Further Evidence

Credit spreads can exhibit extreme volatility. The dotted line of Exhibit 10-6 shows how variable an Aaa credit yield can be. The extreme case took place in the early 1980s when the period-over-period changes rose more than 1½ percentage points in one period and fell roughly 2½ percentage points in the next.

Here, a rising line indicates a reluctance of investors to buy the bonds of these issuers. A falling line indicates increasing willingness to take them. To put this in slightly more technical terms, corporate bonds are priced in terms of a spread over the yield of the current Treasury issue at that maturity. That is, in good times, the market might price the bond of a given corporation at 75 basis points (or three-fourths of a percentage point) over the Treasury yield. In more troubled times, the market might price the bond to yield 150 basis points over the relevant Treasury security. This credit spread indicates how much of a yield premium investors are

Exhibit 10-4 Yield Spread (Moody's Aaa Corporate less Fed Funds Target) versus JOC-ECRI Industrial Price Index (Metals)

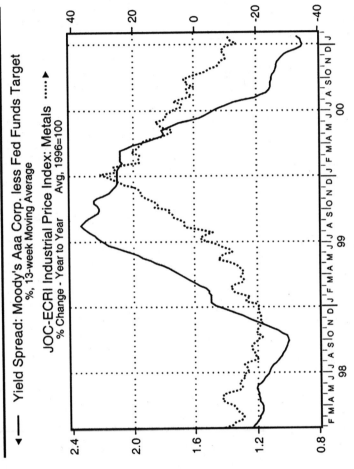

SOURCE: Bureau of Economic Analysis/Haver Analytics

171

Exhibit 10-5 Yield Spread (Moody's Aaa Corporate less Fed Funds) versus JOC-ECRI Industrial Price Index (Metals)

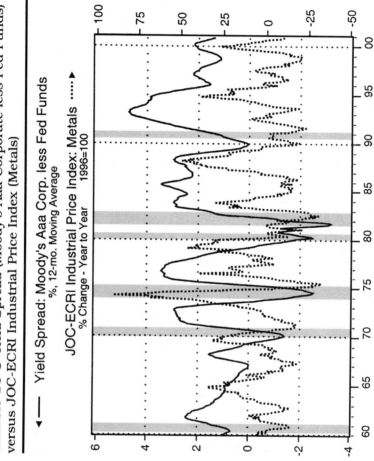

▼—— Yield Spread: Moody's Aaa Corp. less Fed Funds
%, 12-mo. Moving Average

JOC-ECRI Industrial Price Index: Metals ·····▶
% Change - Year to Year   1996=100

SOURCE: Bureau of Economic Analysis/Haver Analytics

Exhibit 10-6 Yield Spread (Moody's Aaa Corporate less Fed Funds) versus Moody's Seasoned Aaa Corporate Bond Yield

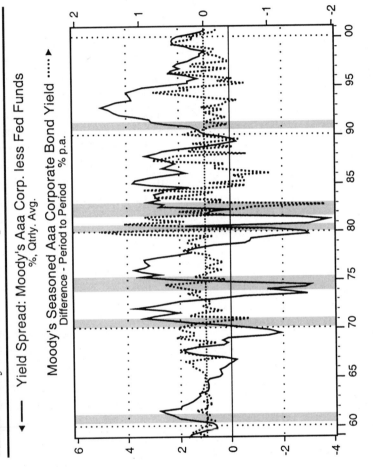

— Yield Spread: Moody's Aaa Corp. less Fed Funds
   %, Qtrly. Avg.

Moody's Seasoned Aaa Corporate Bond Yield ·····▶
   Difference - Period to Period   % p.a.

SOURCE: Bureau of Economic Analysis/Haver Analytics

demanding for taking on the credit risk of the issue. When the credit spread widens, as from 75 to 150 basis points in the example, the bond buyer is saying, in effect, that he or she will lend the money, but it's going to cost more. The dotted line in Exhibit 10-6 shows how this premium has varied during the last 40 years.

Junk bond data are not readily available for comparisons of this kind, but you can easily imagine that if professional investors are growing uneasy about buying Aaa bonds, they must be showing outright alarm at the prospect of buying bonds that are below investment grade—that is, junk bonds.

Still focusing on the 1979–1980 segment of the exhibit, notice that shortly after the yield spread went negative (a sign of an inverted yield curve), the credit spread widened sharply. Two things are true in a case such as this. The yield spread sounded the first warning, and the credit spread corroborated the signal. But, when you see the yield spread narrowing or, worse, inverting and the credit spread widening at the same time, this means that a recession is imminent. You may no longer have 6 months lead time. You had better be ready—with your investments in a defensive position—now.

Assumptions about Investing

The discussion of this chapter makes several assumptions about the broad outlines of your investment plan, even though the details may differ considerably from investor to investor. The first assumption is that you are working with a diversified portfolio. Professional investors have long known that where a holding of one stock might be extremely risky, a holding of several risky stocks, carefully chosen, will comprise a far less risky portfolio. Because this is true, you no doubt hold stocks from a variety of economic sectors.

Further, you have no doubt diversified across such major asset classes as stocks, bonds, and cash. Granted that in the long term you want most of your holdings in stocks and that bonds often seem to detract from overall portfolio performance, at times, bonds may outperform stocks. This was certainly the case in 2000, a year that provided a good reminder of why investment advisors recommend that at least some of your capital go into bonds.

The assumption behind your cash holding is that cash—in the form of a money market fund, Treasury bills, or some such cash equivalent—keeps some of your assets liquid so that you can easily take advantage of opportunities that emerge. Also, there will be times when the markets look too dangerous. The wise move then might be to take yourself out of the game temporarily. During such a time, you can accumulate cash to get ready for better times.

Two further assumptions that seem to go hand in hand are that you want to be fully invested and you want to follow an investment discipline. One of the best features of employee savings plans, such as 401(k) plans, is that you must put a set amount of money to work every pay period. As an individual managing your own portfolio, you should probably do the same thing. As for being fully invested, cash in a money market fund or Treasury bill counts. That cash, after all, is earning at least some return.

Finally, a big part of investment discipline involves an avoidance of overtrading. A good maxim is to buy carefully and sell reluctantly. Financial advisors often point out that in selecting mutual funds, you should look at turnover rates. Funds that trade in and out of holdings too frequently incur huge transaction costs and seldom have good long-term performance records.

One of the saddest recent stories in this regard concerns a day trader who managed to turn a $2.2 million portfolio into a $385,000 portfolio in a year. The newspaper writer reporting this was trying to prove that current technology magnifies market events—especially to the downside. In fact, the relevant benchmark was down 20 percent in 2000, itself a major downturn. The day trader was down over 80 percent. This wasn't technology magnifying what the market was doing to the portfolio. This result is an extreme case of the danger of making far too many trades after far too little thought. Clearly, this kind of trading has no place in the strategic planning of serious investors.

Market Indicators Prompt Asset Allocation Shifts

Study of the yield spread suggests a useful approach to asset allocation among stocks, bonds, and cash. During certain parts of an economic cycle, after all, it may be wise to deemphasize stock while you accumulate cash. At another part of the cycle, you may decide to focus on bonds (more generally, fixed-income securities or mutual funds). Finally, at certain times in the cycle, you may want to bulk up in stocks.

Several rules of thumb can provide a useful basis for deciding when to move from stocks to cash to bonds and back to stocks. Consider Exhibit 10-7, which shows the relationship between the performance of the S&P 500 Index, the standard proxy for the stock market as a whole, and the yield spread.

The dotted line of this exhibit tracks the annual percentage change in the S&P 500 Index. Note that this is not the index level you see every day in the newspaper or on screen but the extent to which the index has changed year over year. The solid line shows the quarterly percentage change in the yield spread.

You can see at a glance that a negative yield spread tends to be negative for stocks. Going back to the late 1960s, you can see that any time the yield spread dropped below the zero line, the performance of this broad market measure ranged from lackluster to bad. In general, a widening yield spread (an upward-moving line) slightly precedes a rising stock market. Once the yield spread peaks, though, it is probably time to start lightening in stocks.

The Conflict between Good Policy and Human Nature

Keep in mind that this tends to be the opposite of what most people do. The response of investors to the offerings of one of the larger mutual fund houses is a case in point. Money poured into these funds in early 2000 because of how well they had done in 1999. These people were buying at the peak. During 2000, though, the funds suffered major losses, and early 2001 saw a major outflow of money fleeing these funds. Now people were selling at or near the bottom. To buy at the peak and then sell at the bottom seems a sure way to lock in a loss.

While it may be human nature to jump on the bandwagon near the end of the parade, it is hardly good investment policy. The strategic approach outlined here more nearly follows the idea of the analyst who said, "This year's bad numbers are next year's great comparisons."

Exhibit 10-7 Yield Spread (Moody's Aaa Corporate less Fed Funds) versus Stock Price Index (S&P's 500 Composite)

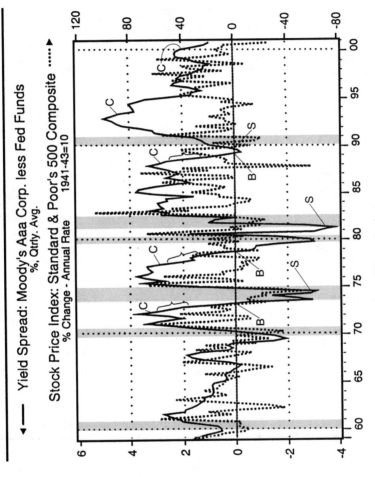

— Yield Spread: Moody's Aaa Corp. less Fed Funds
%, Qtrly. Avg.

Stock Price Index: Standard & Poor's 500 Composite .....▶
% Change - Annual Rate   1941-43=10

SOURCE: Bureau of Economic Analysis/Haver Analytics

Indications of When to Shift Assets

As the spread turns and begins to narrow (a downward-moving line), you may well want to start accumulating cash. The C's in Exhibit 10-7 point to times when investors working within a framework such as this one might have begun the cash accumulation process. The lines pointing to the yield-spread plot are not meant to suggest that this is the exact moment. You could have begun slightly earlier or later.

The lines point to times slightly after the peak to suggest that you need not time your move exactly at the peak. Further, they are meant to emphasize the importance of making sure that the trend has turned and not just paused along the way.

Also, the five moments indicated here are not the only times you might have shifted into cash mode during the decades covered by the exhibit. They are simply representative of the kinds of situations that exist when you should be thinking along these lines.

When the other indicators begin corroborating the message of the yield spread, you may want to start buying bonds. Also, bond yields typically fall sharply early in a recession. It follows that you can get the biggest bang for your buck by going into bonds at, or slightly before, the onset of a recession. Note the three times from 1973 through 1981 marked B. When the yield spread goes negative, you want to have maneuvered your portfolio to have as much commitment to bonds as your investment plan allows. Accordingly, the periods marked with braces (}) would have been good times not only to put money in fixed-income securities but also to put it in longer-maturity securities.

The reason for this is simple. When interest rates fall, fixed-income prices rise. However, while the price of a 5-year security may rise 3.5 percent for every 1 percentage point drop in yields, the price of a 10-year security will increase about 6.5 or 7 percent for every 1 percentage point drop, and the price of a 20- to 30-year security will rise 10 or 12 percent given such a yield drop. Conversely, when interest rates turn upward, fixed-income prices fall, but shorter-maturity securities lose less than longer-maturity securities for a given yield change.

Most individuals must deal with the fixed-income markets through mutual fund intermediaries, of course. Given the way these securities react to interest-rate changes, you need to make sure the fund managers are using strategies that fit in with your sense of what you want to do in this regard.

When the yield spread troughs and turns upward again, you can reverse course and start shifting back into stocks because, as the exhibit shows, these will be relatively better times for stocks. The three points marked S on the exhibit point to three periods, though not the only three, when you could have increased your allocation to stocks. Again, these might not have been the times most people would have chosen. Also, the results might not have been perfect. From the evidence of the exhibit, it looks like anyone working within this framework should have done better than the average investor during these years.

During all these asset allocation shifts, a cautious attitude seems best. One of the keys in this approach is to know when the spread has peaked or troughed. Looking at a display such as the one in Exhibit 10-7 makes it obvious where the peaks and troughs have been. In "real time," these calls are harder to make, and no surefire way exists to know when a market has turned. Indeed, markets often make a few false starts before settling into a new course. Seldom will it be crucial to your financial health to capture the exact moment of the turn. It will usually be enough to capture most of it. A patient and cautious approach may serve you well, hence the emphasis on scaling into and out of positions.

Volatility Can Help You Think about Turning Points

Measures of market volatility can provide helpful information when you are struggling to decide whether the market has settled on a new course.

Suppose that, after a period during which the stock market has taken a beating, you think the yield spread might be starting to widen. Looking at your quote screen, you see that the S&P 500 is trading at 1,200 points, and the screen or your broker provides the information that implied volatility on options on S&P 500 futures has dropped from 22 to 18 percent. This by itself is a good sign, for a falling stock market drives S&P volatility higher, while a rising stock market tends to calm volatility. Further, this volatility decrease tells you that the market pros are revising their estimates of how dangerous the stock market looks at present.

You can also do the volatility arithmetic for, say, 30- and 60-day horizons, as Exhibit 10-8 shows.

You can see from this exercise that with reference to the 30-day horizon, there is a 68 percent probability that the index will lie somewhere between 1138 and 1262 in 30 days and a 95 percent probability that it will lie somewhere between 1076 and 1323. The 60-day horizon extends the ranges, but only slightly. The volatility calculation, then, provides at least a ballpark estimate concerning how much downside the stock market might have left.

Exhibit 10-8 A Volatility Estimate of How Much Downside Is Left

---

1. Divide 365 by the number of days in your time horizon:

$$365/30 = 12.17 \quad 365/60 = 6.08$$

2. Find the square root of that result:

$$\sqrt{12.17} = 3.49 \quad \sqrt{6.08} = 2.47$$

3. Divide the implied volatility by the square root:

$$0.18/3.49 = 0.0516 \quad 0.18/2.47 = 0.0729$$

4. Multiply the index level by that factor:

$$1200 \times 0.0516 = 61.92 \quad 1200 \times 0.0729 = 87.48$$

5. For a 68 percent probability estimate of where the market will be, add that result to, and subtract it from, the current index level:

$$1200 + 61.92 = 1262 \quad 1200 + 87.48 = 1287$$

$$1200 - 61.92 = 1138 \quad 1200 - 87.48 = 1113$$

6. For a 95 percent probability estimate of where the market will be, double the result in step 4 and add it to, and subtract it from, the current index level:

$$1200 + 123.84 = 1324 \quad 1200 + 174.96 = 1375$$

$$1200 - 123.84 = 1076 \quad 1200 - 174.96 = 1025$$

Typical Consumer Behavior Argues for Strategic Discretion

While signs of a slowing economy may alert you to the need to scale back your exposure to the stock market, they do not necessarily mean that you should abandon it. Exhibit 10-9 suggests why this is the case.

This exhibit contrasts personal consumption spending for non-durable and durable goods. The durable goods category includes such things as cars, appliances, and furniture. The nondurable goods category includes food, drugs, gasoline, and clothing. You can see that the solid nondurables line shows far less volatility than the dotted durables line in this exhibit.

When the yield spread narrows, it signals a slowing economy, to be sure. But consider how consumers are likely to respond to worsening economic conditions. They will postpone or cancel discretionary purchases—new houses, cars, appliances, and travel among them. But they will continue to buy food, medicines and medical services, and a variety of other services. In fact, services never go negative.

The contrast between these two categories of consumer spending has obvious implications for your investment strategies. Seeing a slowdown on the way, you may well decide to scale back your exposure to companies that manufacture durable goods or supply materials to those manufacturers. You may be reluctant to alter your holdings of stocks of food, drug, and service providers. These will be hurt less by an economic downturn and may even prosper. If you feel you must buy stocks under these circumstances, the companies involved in nondurable goods and services are probably the ones to think about.

Housing Starts Tell a Similar Story

The comparison of the yield curve with housing starts in Exhibit 10-10 tells a similar story. Housing starts are among the leading indicators, and you can see here that the yield spread often, but not always, leads housing starts by at least 2 or 3 months. The one major anomaly in this picture happened in the late 1980s and early 1990s when, as you know, some other factors interfered with the signals from the market indicators.

Exhibit 10-9 Personal Consumption Expenditures (Nondurable Goods) versus Personal Consumption Expenditures (Durable Goods)

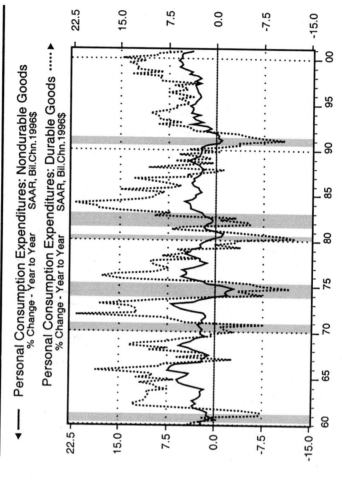

▼——— Personal Consumption Expenditures: Nondurable Goods
% Change - Year to Year   SAAR, Bil.Chn.1996$

Personal Consumption Expenditures: Durable Goods ······▲
% Change - Year to Year   SAAR, Bil.Chn.1996$

SOURCE: Bureau of Economic Analysis/Haver Analytics

Exhibit 10-10 Yield Spread (Moody's Aaa Corporate less Fed Funds) versus Housing Starts

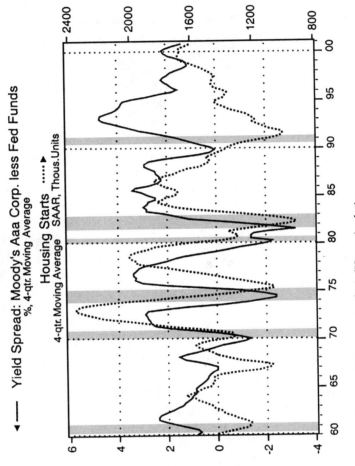

SOURCE: Bureau of Economic Analysis/Haver Analytics

It remains a good generalization that when the yield spread is narrowing, you should get out of stocks related to building supplies and appliances—basically anything that goes into the building and outfitting of new houses.

Obviously, when the yield spread widens, all stocks will do well—because this signals a vibrant and growing economy. Now, though, the stocks of the durable goods makers, including everything related to housing, will shine.

A widening yield spread will also motivate a strong upsurge in business services. Along with this, the conditions that cause the yield spread to widen should create a favorable climate for financial stocks. To see why, consider again that a widening yield spread means that businesses have a strong appetite for credit as they struggle to meet consumer demand. Obviously, then, banks and other financial intermediaries will be busy taking care of these credit needs at a healthy spread over their cost of funds. It follows that their stocks will gain.

A Framework, Not a Final Answer

In conclusion, it seems important to emphasize that despite some of the advertising hype you see, no one has found a sure thing when it comes to investing. This discussion of the market indicators is offered with this caveat very much in mind. Still, to say these market phenomena provide a helpful conceptual and practical framework for your investment planning is to make a strong claim.

Granted, these won't be the only things you will look at. Investing is sufficiently complex and difficult that you need every bit of information you can find from every source available.

Along with the fed funds futures spreads, the yield spread, commodity prices, such credit spreads as the TED and the TAG, and all the other market indicators, you will want to consider the market commentary on a variety of other factors. The traditional economic indicators such as the Consumer Price Index (CPI), the employment numbers, and retail sales can reinforce and corroborate the signals from the market indicators. Turning this around, the market indicators can provide a context for evaluating these economic numbers and the commentary about them.

There can be as many responses to these market signals as there are investors with individual needs, different risk tolerances, and varying amounts of capital to invest. As a result of your continuing study of these market indicators, though, whatever the exact nature of your response, it will be based on reason—not simply a knee-jerk response. And it will be early enough to do you some good.

Glossary

Call: A call option gives the buyer the right, but not the obligation, to buy a specified stock or futures contract for a specified price (the strike or exercise price) within a given period of time. The call buyer, or holder, pays a relatively small price (or premium) for this right. The call seller (or writer) must sell the stock or futures contract at the strike price should the buyer choose to exercise his or her right.

Carry Market: Futures markets offer contracts for delivery during a series of months. For example, the delivery months for stock index and Treasury futures are March, June, September, and December. Energy futures deliver monthly. When the futures prices for a series of months range successively higher, the market is said to be a carry market (an equivalent term is *contango*). The term derives from the fact that price differentials such as these indicate that the market is rewarding storage of the commodity—that is, traders can design a futures trade that will pay at least a large part of the cost of carrying inventory.

Commodity Index: A commodity index, such as the JOC-ECRI, factors together a representative set of commodity prices. In this way, it attempts to provide one number that will gauge overall changes in the costs of all the commodity inputs that the economy requires.

Created Credit: When a central bank pumps new money into the banking system, new credit becomes available. Then people can increase their borrowing and spending without anyone having to forgo spending. As a result, the net buying power of the economy increases (contrast *Transfer Credit*).

Credit Spread: The difference between the yield of a risky fixed-income security such as a corporate bond and a default risk-free Treasury security of similar maturity is known as a credit spread. It represents the price of the actuarial risk of default on that debt.

Delta: Option prices change in a ratio to changes in the price of the underlying stock or futures contract. The delta of an option identifies this ratio. Deltas range between 0 and 1 for calls and between 0 and −1 for puts. A delta of 0.50 indicates that the price of the option will change 50 cents for every dollar change in the price of the stock. A delta of 0.31 indicates that the option price will change 31 cents for every dollar change in the price of the stock. The delta of an option also approximates the probability that the option will expire in the money.

Economic Indicators: Various departments of the federal government and other official agencies compile economic data such as housing starts, the Consumer Price Index (CPI), and employment data. These are grouped into leading, coincident, and lagging indicators. Obviously, leading indicators are those which have proved to precede economic events, while coincident indicators emerge at the same time and lagging indicators after the fact. The weaknesses of these indicators include their dependence on government sources, the time lapse required to compile and distribute the data, and the frequency of miscalculations and revisions. Because of all this, interpretation of these data takes considerable expertise and leaves room for disagreement among analysts concerning what a given set of data may mean.

Fed Funds Rate: The term refers to the interest rates charged when bank members of the Federal Reserve system borrow and lend reserves among themselves, usually on an overnight basis. In fact, there are many such rates because a lender of reserves will change according to the creditworthiness of the borrowing bank. However, the Federal Reserve Bank of New York compiles a fed effective rate that averages the actual rates to provide a useful benchmark for this cost of credit.

Futures: Futures are standardized, exchange-traded contracts for future delivery of a variety of physical and financial commodities. These contracts define the commodity or index and specify the size of the trading unit, the form of price quotation, and the method of final settlement. Only the price is open to negotiation. Because this price negotiation takes place in a regulated public marketplace, it distills the knowledge and opinions of a large number of market users into one price. This price represents what people are willing to pay "now" for future delivery.

Historical Volatility: An historical volatility figure indicates how variable a market has been during a specified period in the immediate past. Depending on the source, it is possible to see volatilities ranging from 10- to 100-day figures. Basically, to arrive at a 10-day volatility, analysts perform a statistical analysis on day-to-day price changes for the last 10 days and express the result in annualized percentage terms. A 10 percent volatility claims a two-thirds probability (plus or minus 1 standard deviation) that 1 year from the day of the reading the price of the stock or futures contract will lie in a range plus or minus 10 percent of the current price. That is, if the current price is 100, a 10 percent volatility claims a two-thirds probability that the price 1 year from now will lie somewhere between 90 and 110.

Implied Volatility: Volatility is a key factor in the determination of option prices. Often, though, an option price varies from what the historical volatility suggests it should be. This price implies a volatility other than the historical—hence the term. Volatility tends to revert to its mean value, so another way to look at implied volatility is as a market estimate of the long-term mean.

Interest Rate: An interest rate defines the cost of credit. These vary according to whether the loan is secured by collateral, the term to maturity of the credit instrument, and also the creditworthiness of the borrower. Normally, a lender will charge more for an unsecured loan than for one secured by collateral. Similarly, all else the same, the cost for a 10-year loan will be greater than for a 5-year loan. And a lesser credit will have to pay more than a better credit.

Inverted Market: Futures markets offer contracts for delivery during a series of months. For example, the delivery months for stock index and Treasury futures are March, June, September, and December. Energy futures deliver monthly. When the futures prices for a series of months range successively lower, the market is said to be an inverted market (an equivalent term is *backwardated*). Price differentials such as these indicate that the market is experiencing a supply shortage, or that there is the perception of shortage, and is rewarding the immediate delivery of goods and penalizing the storage of them.

Inverted Yield Curve: When shorter-term yields are higher than longer-term yields, the yield curve has inverted. This typically portends a recession or, at least, a period of slower economic growth.

Market: In the sense of the discussion of this book, a market is a group of people exchanging information and opinions through a process of bidding and offering. The group can gather in a centralized marketplace like a stock exchange or a board of trade, or it can be widely scattered and communicate electronically. What matters is that the price on which all these people settle at any moment represents the sum of all these people's thinking and opinions about the commodity, interest-rate instrument, or stock index or option in question.

Market Indicators: A market indicator is a price or yield spread or relationship that has proved to have predictive value—to be, in effect, a leading indicator. The fed funds futures spreads, yield curves, and commodity price indexes and spreads are typical examples. The advantages of market indicators include their ready availability, ease of interpretation, and definitiveness or lack of revision. These market data gain additional value from the fact that they incorporate the knowledge and viewpoints of large numbers of people.

Normal Yield Curve: When longer-term yields are higher than shorter-term yields, the yield curve is normal. An equivalent term is an upwardly sloping yield curve. This typically portends a period of more rapid economic growth.

Options: These are financial contracts that give buyers of calls the right to buy and buyers of puts the right to sell a specified item at a certain price for an agreed-upon period of time. In neither case is the option buyer obliged to do so. In everyday life, car insurance offers a good example of a put option. The holder of a complete replacement policy has the right to sell a specified car to the insurance company for its full price any time during the life of the policy, regardless of what has happened to the car. A store sale rain check is essentially a call that gives the customer the right to the sale price of an item at another time. In either case the option holder will exercise the right only if it makes economic sense to do so.

Price Spreads: Quotation services ordinarily list futures prices for a number of contract months. The spreads are the month-to-month price differences. As indicators, the array of spreads for a commodity such as gasoline or for an interest rate such as the fed funds rate can provide valuable clues about how the market sees the supply-demand relationship for the period in question. Thus the price spreads provide a kind of term structure that can be usefully forward looking.

Put: A put option gives the buyer the right, but not the obligation, to sell a specified stock or futures contract for a specified price (the strike or exercise price) within a given period of time. The put buyer, or holder, pays a relatively small price (or premium) for this right. The put seller (or writer) must buy the stock or futures contract at the strike price should the buyer choose to exercise his or her right.

Refining Spread: This spread uses futures contracts on crude oil, unleaded gasoline, and heating oil to approximate the gross return to petroleum refining and so to capture the economics of refining. The traditional term for this relationship is the *crack spread* because refiners speak in terms of cracking out the various products, and the tall, narrow towers that distinguish refinery skylines are cracking towers.

Spread: In market language, this term has several senses. The one that matters most for this discussion refers to the difference between two prices or yields for different contract months or different points on the yield curve. For example, the January-February fed funds spread identifies the difference between the prices or yields for two contract months. The fed funds–10-year Treasury-note spread identifies the difference between the yields at two points along the yield curve.

Stock Index: A collection of stocks designed to track the performance of the entire market or of a market sector. The most commonly referred to indexes are the Standard and Poor's (S&P) 500 Index and the Dow Jones Industrial Average. Because these portfolios have long track records to demonstrate their reliability, changes in these portfolios can be said to index changes in the market as a whole.

TAG Spread: This spread identifies the price difference between a 10-year Treasury security and an agency security of similar maturity. Thus it identifies the market estimate of this credit spread. The advantage of this credit-spread indicator is that the presence of futures contracts on both sides makes it easy to keep track of.

TED Spread: Another credit spread, the TED identifies the price difference between a risk-free Treasury and a risky Eurodollar deposit. The original TED focused on 3-month maturities. More recently, the focus has shifted to longer-term relationships. The most commonly traded term TEDs are the 2- and the 5-year.

Term Structure: The most common use of this phrase is with reference to a yield curve, which structures yields at different terms to maturity. It is also possible to think about commodity prices in this way. In this case, the term structure, instead of relating yields to maturities, relates prices to futures delivery months.

Transfer Credit: When a person or institution lends to another person or institution, the net buying power of the economy stays the same. The lender gives up buying power so the borrower can buy something. Accordingly, this extension of credit results in a transfer of buying power (contrast *Created Credit*).

Volatility: This term has both informal and technical uses. Informally, if the stock market, say, bounces up and down 150 or 200 points a day for several days, it is said to be a volatile market. Technically, market users can measure past price or yield changes (compare *Historical Volatility*) or estimate the future magnitude of price or yield changes (compare *Implied Volatility*).

Yield: The annualized total rate of return from both interest payments and capital change for a fixed-income security is its yield to maturity. This is the yield commonly referred to in yield curves and in the pricing of fixed-income securities.

Yield Curve: A graph showing the relationships of yields at different maturities is a yield curve. An equivalent term is the *term structure* of yields. The most commonly cited yield curve is the U.S. Treasury yield curve, but quotation services also provide curves for other countries and for other kinds of fixed-income securities such as corporate bonds.

About the Authors

Paul Kasriel, director of economic research for The Northern Trust Company, is responsible for making the corporation's economic and interest-rate forecasts. Through his economic and financial commentaries, Kasriel has developed a loyal following in the financial community. He is often quoted in national publications including *Barron's, BusinessWeek, Investor's Business Daily,* and *The New York Times,* and he has appeared on CNN, CNBC, and PBS.

Keith Schap is a writer in the market and product development department of the Chicago Board of Trade. Previously a senior editor with *Futures* magazine, where he developed market outlooks for numerous markets, Schap has contributed over 300 articles to magazines and journals including *Futures, Treasury and Risk Management,* and *Derivative Strategies.*

Index